1000 ideas for term papers in SOCIOLOGY

by the editors of Arc Books

ARC BOOKS
New York

An ARC BOOK
published by Arco Publishing Company, Inc.
219 Park Avenue South,
New York, N.Y. 10003

Library of Congress Catalog Number 78-80883
Printed in the United States of America

Contents

Preface

MANY students fear term papers and feel that they are designed solely to drag them down from a good to a disappointing grade. Although this idea is false, it is true that term papers require more real thinking and reveal the student more accurately than exams do. An exam takes but a few hours of writing and thinking, whereas a term paper can require from three weeks to three months of hard thinking, diligent research, and precise composition. More importantly, even a term paper on an assigned subject gives the student more freedom of thought than he has with a strictly limited exam question; and such freedom can easily lead straight into pitfalls. With a term paper on a topic of your own choice, the freedom to damn or to save yourself is absolute. It is natural to regard such papers with dread.

If you have a good topic, organized research and writing, and average intelligence, there is absolutely no reason to fear term papers. Yet a good topic can be hard to find, and organized research and writing do not come naturally. Thus we present in this book a comprehensive selection of detailed topics and a working guide to efficient research and effective academic writing. You must supply only your intelligence, and if you have doubts about that, forget them—you would not be in school in the first place if you were not blessed with at least average intelligence. Besides, as the saying goes, "Writing is 99 per cent perspiration and 1 per cent inspiration," and this book should help you eliminate most of the perspiration. If you use it properly, you will find that term papers really are nothing to worry about.

One word of caution: to use this book well, be sure to read it all the way through, rather than skipping to the second section, which contains our collection of topics. Even if you are pressed for time and would like to find a topic immediately so you can start work at once, resist the temptation. The few minutes you spend reading our suggestions on research and writing will save you many wasted hours in the library and at the typewriter. And such guidance will help you to write a better paper no matter what topic you finally choose.

PART I
A SHORT GUIDE TO THE ART OF TERM PAPER WRITING

Introduction

EVERY student has been confronted with the necessity of writing a term paper. This often produces anxiety. The student may become confused about what topic to write on. Once he has found a topic, he may find his research has gotten out of hand and when he sits down before the typewriter, set on writing a first draft, he may discover he is unable to write a clear and intelligible paper.

The foregoing need not happen. The surest way to success is simply to put things into perspective. First determine how long the paper should be, or, if its length is not specified, how much time you are willing to spend on it. Find out at the same time what kind of paper is expected, whether it should be a comparatively simple report or something more complex, like a thoughtful analysis of several theories. Once you have an idea of what the paper should be, you are now ready to put into perspective its various stages, assigning specific periods of time for each of the four large phases of production—finding a topic, doing research, organizing materials and developing ideas, and writing. It is vital that you be precise about the time you will spend on each phase. That is the only way to avoid the massive confusion and despair that accompany the realization that research, for example, has taken nineteen days, leaving only two days for the equally important phases of organization, development and writing. By keeping each phase separate and confined to its own time period, you will escape that chilling combination of phases which leaves you still trying to define a topic when you should be writing. In short, avoid writing a poor term paper by getting perspective on your paper, breaking it down into phases, assigning clear and strict periods of time to each phase, and adhering to that schedule.

This book is designed to be helpful in the processes of definition and division. Only you can say how much time you should devote to each phase, as this varies according to the conditions of specific term papers and to your characteristics as a writer. (Very generally, though, finding a topic and doing research take as long as organizing, developing, and writing.) We have provided one chapter for each phase, and these chapters appear in their correct order, beginning with "The Search for a Topic" and ending with "Term Paper Tips." Each chapter contains a general discussion of the phase, definitions and explanations of each step within a phase, and instructions on the best way of taking these steps. If you combine our detailed chapters with your own effort, your paper will be manageable, orderly, easier to write, and, above all, worthy of your talents. With a little application and a rational approach, you will avoid term paper disaster.

Because selecting a topic is the first phase, it affects every succeeding one, yet it can be terribly difficult to do properly. It requires much thought and precision. Therefore we have included an eleborate chapter on this phase as well as a large and varied compendium of topics, each of which is treated in detail. When you have finished the chapters of Part I, refer to this compendium. Even if you have a topic clearly in mind, our list can give you valuable ideas for your own topic and show you how to give it workable form.

Finally, remember that a term paper is a very personal affair. It is the clearest possible expression of your ability to think in an original yet orderly way. We can help you to do this with a minimum of pain and wasted effort, but the end product will be your very own, and so you should feel free to change our suggestions to suit your individual methods, as long as those methods work.

CHAPTER 1

The Search for a Topic

IT is impossible to overstress the importance of choosing the right topic. The decisions you make during this first phase will have profound effects on every succeeding phase of production. A topic that is too abstruse will leave you rushing about to find nonexistent materials during the research phase; one which is too vague, too large, too small, or too fanciful will lead to serious problems of organization and development; and a topic that bores you or seems too difficult will undermine all your efforts at writing, no matter how thoroughly you have researched, organized, and developed the material. The right topic—one of reasonable difficulty, size, importance, and, especially, interest—will support every phase of paper development and significantly lighten what can be a crushing task. There are few, if any, ideal topics, but a little care in choosing always will lead you to one that suits your paper; and there is a reliable method for finding and refining such topics.

The first step is to find an *area of concern*. As sociology is a broad discipline and subsumes hosts of other fields, these areas of concern must be quite general. You will find a full list of areas of concern in sociology in the introduction to Part II of this book; among them are headings like "The Individual and Society," "Social Change," and "Society in Historical and Comparative Perspective." These are broad titles for a number of sociological concerns, many of which might be appropriate to several areas; but when they are grouped together, such concerns as the life-cycle, childhood, and social deviance seem to be summarized best by one heading—"The Individual and Society." This heading includes the *essence* of each of those concerns. All three could be approached from another area of concern, but none of them could be contained within another area as completely as they are within "The Individual and Society."

Although areas of concern are general, be as definite as you can when choosing one. Think long and hard about those aspects of sociology which are both interesting to you and relevant to your paper, choose one area, and stick to it despite all temptations to switch. Uncertainty in choosing an area almost always leads to dangerous interpenetration. Specify, for example, whether you want to write about "The Origins of Society" or "Social Psychology and Group Behavior" even though your deepest interest may involve both areas. Once you have made a definite choice, you will be able to approach even a complex topic involving several areas, for you then will have a real starting point and a primary emphasis, both of which are important for clarity. If you do not make a definite choice, your area of concern may expand to humanity itself, which is the very broadest concern of sociology.

Sometimes the course for which you are writing the paper will delineate an area of concern for you. Yet your range of choice remains broad, for the seemingly divergent areas of sociology all have something to say to one another. For a course dealing with contemporary funeral rites, for example, the prime area of concern would seem to be "Social Structure and Institutions," but you could relegate that area to second place and begin with "Society in Historical and Comparative Perspective." The only important thing is relevance. If you keep this quality in mind, you can choose any area of concern and any topic you wish to. You even could write about apes for a group behavior course if you can tie it in by making parallels and contrasts between primate rituals like presenting and human ways of dealing with leadership, challengers, and supporters.

Even if you are unfamiliar with the structure of sociology, it is easy to find an area of concern that interests you. Lectures, reading assignments, and course titles themselves offer useful guidance. The areas we have listed in Part II, of course, will be the easiest to find and to understand, for each is followed by a large group of appropriate topics. Still, you need not depend on our listing if you are confident enough to look for yourself. You are sure to find an exciting area of concern; and if it differs semantically from the ones we have listed, it easily can be related to them.

The next two steps in your search for a topic are to choose a *general topic* within your area of concern and to *adopt an approach* to that topic. These steps are largely interdependent—one can lead to another. Which step you decide to take first depends on the requirements of your paper and on your personal predilections. For some people, it may be of paramount importance to approach the topic of pygmy family structure in any way possible; for others, the reverse is true—they would prefer to use an analytic approach to any aspect of primitive culture. In the first example, the general topic takes precedence over the approach; the second case is a decision in favor of one approach over any general topic. Remember, however you begin, the steps will influence each other.

Unless you are taking a methodological course (something like "Sociological Applications of Statistics"), you probably will begin by selecting a general topic. How general depends on several factors. Estimates of the length of your paper and of the time you are willing to spend on it will be very important here. The smaller the paper, and the less the time you want to spend, the more specific your general topic must be. Given a two-hundred page paper and eight months, however, your general topic would have to be rather large.

Also consider your mode of approach. Certain general topics are more suited to one approach than to others. A particular behavioral question can best be answered by a laboratory approach, something which would be entirely useless for an overview of several theoretical works.

The depth of your approach is as important as the mode. If your approach is exhaustive—rigorous experiments, for example—then you will need a highly specific general topic. Less rigorous experiments, perhaps conducted on the street rather than in the laboratory, call for broader general topics.

Finally, you should check your general topic against the paper's requirements. Does it meet them? Is it directly relevant to the course, and can you foresee how it will tie in with the course after you have developed it and written the paper? Checking for relevance is important at all times;

it precludes a stunning revelation at the last minute that all your work is completely useless; and it is especially vital when choosing a general topic.

Having chosen a general topic, you will adopt an approach to that topic. What approach again depends on factors like time and energy. You simply cannot choose an elaborate approach like original data collection if your time is limited; in this case, a library research paper or comparative book report will be more successful. Secondly, consider your training and prejudices. While the hard core scientist may not write as good an historical analysis as the social historian, he certainly will write a better experimental report. Carefully assess your talents and skills to find an approach that complements them.

Lastly, make sure your approach is compatible with your general topic and with the course for which you are writing the paper. You may have stumbled on an inherently inappropriate combination of approach and topic, trying to use behavioral experiments, for example, to criticize advanced social theories. Such an undertaking may not prove absolutely impossible, but it will be needlessly difficult to complete, and your conclusions will be unsatisfying and shaky. Checking how well the approach suits the course makes even more sense; an unsuitable approach may not seriously affect the validity of your paper, but it can prejudice your reader unfavorably. Some courses naturally encourage all sorts of approaches, but be sure yours is one of them before you make any definite decisions.

You may find it difficult to think of all the approaches that are open to you. As this deficiency can cheat you of an excellent topic-approach combination, we have provided an example of the six major ways to treat most topics.

Let us suppose that your area of concern is "Social Structure and Institutions" and that your general topic is "Bureaucracy." Here are six possible approaches to that general topic:

1. *Library Research Using Secondary Sources*
   Survey three or four major interpretations of bureaucracy. State what each author says, how he comes to say it (his methods and references), the circumstances of his interpretation (biographical and social), the relevance of the respective theories (to yourself, to interpreting our time, etc.) and try to rate these theories according to your own criteria.

2. *Data Collection—Survey and Observation*
   Choose an institution that you can penetrate and that qualifies as a formal organization. Place yourself within it as an observer and take notes in order to compare the formal, official chain of command (as stated in the charter, rules, etc.) with the informal organization, the networks of solidarity and conflict, and the unwritten codes of behavior. You also might conduct informal interviews. Use your data to suggest or to generate an hypothesis.

3. *Theoretical—Analysis*
   Examine in detail one theory of formal organizations (Weber's, Blau's, or Crozier's). Derive a set of hypotheses or assumptions for the theory. Test these by referring to recent research in professional journals.

Theoretical—Synthesis

Examine two or three theories of formal organizations. Specify the gaps that separate them. Using recent research to supplement your thinking, suggest how these gaps might be bridged or eliminated.

4. *Interdisciplinary*

   Apply one conceptual framework of bureaucracy to the interpretation of a literary work. Choose a book like Balzac's *The Civil Servants* or Kafka's *The Castle* and reformulate its contents in sociological terms.

5. *Pop*

   Specify popular, pejorative concepts of bureaucracy. How do they appear in mass media, in a television program like *The Doctors* or in a movie like *Alice's Restaurant*? Compare these concepts with generally accepted facts about bureaucracies, and try to specify what needs the popular image fulfills.

6. *Experimental*

   Select two groups of subjects essentially similar in age, background, education, etc. Ask both groups to perform a certain task, but organize one rigidly, leaving little or no room for individual initiative. Designate a chain of command and distribute duties clearly among members of this group. Let the other group organize itself. Give it a looser atmosphere. Then compare individual performance within each group and try to specify how it is affected by bureaucratic structure. You might also change the nature of the task to see if performance varies with the kind of work to be done.

It should be clear that each approach is varied. *Library Research* also could be a comparison of two or more descriptive works or a synthesis of such books. *Data Collection* might use statistical surveys, observations, interviews, and data collected by others, and the *Interdisciplinary* approach might call for applying sociology to economics instead of literature. Sociology gives you great flexibility in choosing a topic and developing an approach.

This flexibility may be confusing when it comes to preparing and writing your paper. Having chosen a general topic and approach, how can you know precisely what to look for when you begin to do library research or to set up an experiment? The best way is to take the fourth step of selecting a topic—*narrowing*. Once you have developed a feasible, definite topic-approach combination, focus on a particular aspect or example of that combination. If you have chosen to do a library research paper on childhood conditioning, you might concentrate on using studies of teenage gangs and of the urban family to see how the absence of a *rite de passage* contributes to rebellion in contemporary American society. With a definite approach and specific topic like this, you will find that research is easy, pleasant, and even exciting. Best of all, refining your topic and approach gives your paper a central thrust that will carry it through from introduction to conclusion with admirable unity. The student who does not take this fourth step often finds that he must do so when writing the conclusion to his paper, when it is too late to do him any good.

To narrow your topic-approach intelligently, you will have to look in different places for particular ideas. If you are doing the paper on childhood conditioning, you can start narrowing by preliminary research. Look in a general text like Erikson's *Childhood and Society,* which should give you at least four or five good specific ideas. Pay special attention to any narrow studies that the author cites as evidence for his general conclusions, for you easily might borrow the topic of such a study, treating it in your own way, or criticize the study itself. Do not disdain specialized encyclopedias, bibliographies, and periodicals, for you never can tell where you will find a specific topic and a narrow approach to go with it.

Other fertile sources of ideas include talking with your professor about your general topic and asking for specific suggestions, picking over assigned readings that are relevant to your topic, and re-reading lecture notes to glean the names of particular aspects of a topic that was mentioned in passing. Bear in mind the limits you applied to the first three steps of your search for a topic—time, space, and expertise. These will help you to skirt ideas that are blind alleys. Also, you can ease the process of research and development by exploring the limitations of the material. The available resources may be too few to support your topic, in which case you will save yourself the trouble of frantic searches during the research phase by exploring those limitations now.

Finally, ask yourself the same questions you have been asking all along: Is your topic relevant to your course, to the kind of paper that the course requires, and to some major concern of sociology? Is it relevant to *you*—do you care about it? Will it permit you to do the kind of paper you want to do within the limits of resources, time, effort, and personal ability? Are the topic and approach specific enough to keep your research and thinking within reasonable boundaries? If the answer to all these questions is "yes," then you are sure to have a superior topic.

Admittedly, the seach for a topic as we have described it is not the casual undertaking that most people suppose. It takes time, research and hard thinking. It is rigorous and fairly difficult. But beyond the negative advantages of avoiding term paper disaster, wasted time, and misspent effort, there are great positive advantages; for once you have completed a thorough search for a topic, the rest of your work in writing a term paper is almost done. In that search you have discovered exactly what you will write on and precisely how you will write about it; you have acquired a usefully clear notion of the references you will use and of the thesis you will propound. If your search has been a good one, you also will have a rough idea of what the parts of your paper should look like, from introduction to conclusion. In short, the search for a topic has produced a comprehensive plan for your paper; you need only fill in the blanks of research, development, and writing. Your paper already exists in essence.

CHAPTER 2

Research Sources

THOSE who have ever tried to write a sociology term paper will know that, in contrast to most fields, sociology overflows with sources for research. The real problem is not how to find enough material, but how to limit your quest for sources. If you fail to take steps to limit your research, you may never finish it.

The first thing to do is to familiarize yourself thoroughly with the library or libraries at your disposal. Despite all the efforts of the Library of Congress and various library associations, each library has its own peculiarities of classification and organization. So it is unsafe to presume that if you have seen one library, you have seen them all. Such an attitude might lead you to ignore fertile sources or to search fruitlessly for important works. Before you even think of beginning the preliminary research that will accompany your search for a topic, be sure that you know your library well. Visit and examine the reference room, the card catalogs, the periodical room, any reserve rooms or special libraries, and the stacks. While there, test your understanding of how the materials are arranged. Are all journals and other periodicals stored in bound volumes in one place, or are some years bound and other years left loose at another location? How are reference works arranged—by subject or by type of work (*i.e.*, dictionaries, bibliographies, etc.)? Do special libraries or rooms have their own catalog, and do their classification systems parallel those of the main library? Do you understand clearly how reserve books are arranged?

After you have acquainted yourself with the physical layout of your library, explore its theoretical structure—the card catalog and other centralized classification schemes. Many libraries classify periodicals in a special way—sometimes a circular file—so it pays to be very careful in looking over the classification schemes. The same holds true for reserve and reference books in many cases.

Some larger libraries issue various pamphlets about their catalogs, stacks, and special sections. These can be helpful, but your ultimate source of guidance is the librarian, especially in smaller libraries. The librarian usually has years of experience in coping with the frequently complicated organization and procedures of a particular library or section thereof; and that experience is yours for the asking. Do not be afraid to inquire. Librarians recognize that one of their most important duties is to make the library accessible to the aspiring student.

The best sociology reference work is *Sources of Information in the Social Sciences*, by Carl M. White and Associates (Totowa, New Jersey: Bedminster Press, 1964). Chapter 4 of White's book is entirely devoted to listing and briefly describing the major theoretical, statistical, observational, encyclopedic, and periodical reference sources in the field of sociology. Other chapters cover related areas like social psychology, economics, and history. Once you have mastered library mechanics, find a copy of this compendium. As you proceed through the four steps of finding the right topic, you will find the sources listed in White's book will help you by throwing light on major sociological concerns.

Also helpful at this general stage is the *International Encyclopedia of the Social Sciences,* edited by David L. Sills (New York: Macmillan, 1968). Published in seventeen volumes, this work covers every conceivable topic, author, and major treatise in sociology and related fields. In it you will find detailed articles on men like Weber, Marx, Simmel, and Durkheim, all of whose work did much to shape sociology. These articles isolate the principal concerns of these men, describe the development of their thought, and provide complete bibliographies.

Among the more valuable sources for general and specific information to guide your choice of topic and area of research are the following:

Thematic Summaries

Current Sociology by UNESCO (London: Blackwell, published quarterly) provides summaries and examinations of contemporary trends in sociology. It examines different topics each year and includes extensive bibliographic references. If you have any idea at all about your topic, look in *Current Sociology* for suggestions. *A Handbook of Sociology* by Ogburn and Nimkoff (Boston: Houghton Mifflin, 1958) reviews and explains seven broad areas of sociology. A general index to sociological concerns and a bibliography selected because of its relevance to those concerns appear also.

Bibliographies

The *International Bibliography of Social Research* by UNESCO (Chicago: Aldine, published annually) lists sources of original work by author and by subject. All sorts of sociological works from all countries are included. For more specialized bibliographies (in social psychology, for example) refer both to *Sources of Information in the Social Sciences* and to the *Bibliographic Index*, which lists bibliographies in every academic discipline.

Periodical Indices

Sociological Abstracts (New York, five times a year) gives brief summaries of articles in more than two-hundred-fifty magazines. It also carries complete indices for more than two dozen periodicals that are relevant to sociology. Abstracts appear under subject headings, so this publication is easy to use as a source for topics, and for recent studies to support your arguments. Other articles that appeared in a variety of magazines can be found in *The Reader's Guide to Periodical Literature* and in *Poole's Index to Periodical Literature*. Do not forget that many articles you might use for illustration or analysis appear in popular magazines or in periodicals seemingly unrelated to sociology.

Data Collections

Statistics can suggest a topic, and they certainly are essential to many kinds of sociological studies. Fortunately, there are several good collections of population statistics. The United Nations Statistical Office publishes an annual called the *Demographic Yearbook.* It contains statistical summaries of population size and characteristics for every country in the world. Similar statistics for the United States alone (and in greater detail) appear in the *Statistical Abstract of the United States,* compiled by the United States Bureau of the Census (Washington: U.S. Government Printing Office, annually). For more general world information, the United Nations also publishes a *Statistical Yearbook.* For information of great use in historical surveys and analyses, the United States Bureau of the Census publishes *Historical Statistics of the United States, Colonial Times to 1957* (Washington: U.S. Government Printing Office, 1960).

Dictionaries

When writing theoretical papers, you may need good definitions of sociological terms, for the field constantly is expanding. New theories, methods, and terms arise frequently. Two sources of such information are *A Dictionary of Sociology* by Henry P. Fairchild (New York: Philosophical Library, 1944) and *A Glossary of Sociological Terms* by Clement S. Mihanovich (Milwaukee: Bruce, 1957).

Periodicals

As you might imagine, new sociological journals emerge annually. So many now exist that it is wiser to consult a periodical index than to go directly to files of sociological periodicals. Yet two of them are leaders in the field and have shown longevity: the *American Journal of Sociology,* published bi-monthly by the University of Chicago Press, and the *American Sociological Review*, published bi-monthly in New York by the American Sociological Association. Simply thumbing through back issues of these publications will suggest many good topics; and when you come to doing full-fledged research, you will find that articles appearing in these journals are invaluable.

The preceding list should help you to get your research underway with little trouble. Yet some kinds of papers (like data collection and experimental studies) require more than library research; they involve scientific methods with which you may be unfamiliar and procedures which need clarification. If you are doing such a paper, be sure to look at *The Language of Social Research* by Lazarsfeld and Rosenberg (Glencoe, Ill: The Free Press, 1955). This book describes in detail the proper methods for conducting quantitative research in sociology. If your paper involves the case approach to sociology, refer to Matilda Riley's *Sociological Research* (New York: Harcourt, Brace and World, 1963). For all papers that demand original investigation, the classic methodological guide is Goode and Hatt's *Methods in Social Research* (New York: McGraw, 1952).

Depending on the kind of paper you are writing, theoretical guidance may be more important than methodological instruction. It is difficult to do a theoretical analysis without a thorough grounding in the hypotheses with which you are working. If you want a general orientation in social theory, see Talcott Parsons' *Theories of Society* (New York: Free Press of Glencoe, 1961). This two volume work is truly comprehensive and should answer all your questions. Equally valuable in its own way is Gardner Lindzey's *Handbook of Social Psychology* (Cambridge, Mass.: Addison-Wesley, 1954). More limited than the Parsons book, it is clear enough to be of real help to those who are confused about the bases of many sociological theories.

No matter what sources you approach, pay attention to footnotes. No scholarly book, no prestigious periodical article, and no genuinely valuable handbook can do without footnotes. They are the author's intellectual pedigree and are supposed to certify the solidity (if not the validity) of his work. They are also a genuine boon to the student, for footnotes can offer a large number of ideas for topics. And because a footnote occurs in context, it gives the student a general idea of the content and approach of the work cited, thus saving him the time usually needed to locate, obtain, and generally assess a book whose character is unknown. In practical terms, a footnote can lead you to a particular work or sharply focused study you might analyze or criticize; it can indicate a good reference for your own thesis; or it can help you to analyze the work at hand by studying its antecedents and supportive studies.

Bibliographies, of course, are as integral to a scholarly paper or book as footnotes are. A bibliography has one disadvantage in comparison to a footnote: the substance and form of the work listed usually are not as clear, for there is no context to indicate them. The best bibliographies often include a capsule description of listed works; but all bibliographies do have an advantage absent from footnotes—the information is presented in a summary, rather than sprinkled throughout the text, and thus is better adapted to a streamlined research effort.

It is advisable to use footnotes and bibliographical references with discretion; remember that indiscriminate use of these tools will sabotage your efforts. It will lead you in an endless spiral with a radically increasing diameter. The number of works you consult can increase geometrically—one book will lead you to three others, those three to nine more, and so forth—unless you are ruthless. Always ask, "Do I really *need* this work? Is it so solid, relevant, and provocative as to be undeniably necessary"? Unless your answer is an unequivocal and enthusiastic affimative, pass quickly over the reference and spend your time on more rewarding works. Researching a term paper is a specific task with a definite goal, not an exercise in general education.

Finally, consider living rather than printed sources of information. If yours is a theoretical paper, consider writing to the proponent of a theory, or to one of its major supporters; if you have clear questions about a research paper, do not hesitate to ask them of the paper's author. The world of scholarship, after all, is supposed to be founded on intellectual give and take. If your man is available locally, a personal interview is most profitable; if he is not, be sure to pay close attention to your letter requesting information. Verify that your questions are specific and make sense. Indicate the nature of your paper as impressively as possible without being pompous or vague. If you can get permission to use your sociology department's stationery, do so; busy scholars and administrators naturally are inclined to pay attention to requests that seem important and officially sanctioned. The same holds true for government leaders, artists, journalists, and all the other living sources that your paper may require. Be precise, unabashed, and impressive, and your chances of a useful reply are very high.

Do not overlook the value of talking with other sociology students and with intellectually competent friends. You can use all the help you can get, especially if you are doing an original survey or trying to explore a topic in pop sociology. The intellectual interplay of such talks can uncover previously unknown works, primary sources, and approaches. As long as you avoid "bull sessions" and realize that every minute of your time is valuable, directed conversations can be useful. Beware in such cases of letting things degenerate into generality and irrelevance.

The kinds and numbers of research sources that you decide to use depend on the nature of your paper. A laboratory or observation paper usually requires fewer references than a synthesis or a theoretical exploration, but this is not always the case. Similarly, there is a great distinction between the kinds of sources used for a secondary and for a primary paper. Those for the former are fairly limited. Mainly they will be the writings and researches of others. For a primary paper, however, the major source might be interviews conducted by the writer while a basic methodological or theoretical work could be the only source written by another.

In estimating the number of sources you should use, observe only one rule—sources alone do not make a paper. If you can write a well-reasoned, valid and meaningful paper with only one or two sources, it makes no sense to clutter your work with references you do not need. If your arguments require ten or twelve references, use them by all means. But no matter how many references you use, they cannot disguise a poorly conceived and executed paper. References may document the bases of your thought, lend support to your arguments or demonstrate your awareness of the major trends in a field; but they are no substitute for original thinking.

CHAPTER 3

Organization and Development

WHEN you have found the right topic and mapped out the research territory, you now are ready to begin the actual construction of your paper. For the most part, this will be a pleasant rather than an arduous task. If you have completed the preceding stages with care, construction will seem like the natural and inevitable realization of the ideas and relationships that were implicit in your topic from the beginning. The only real difficulty at this point is to organize the thoughts that you discover and the points that come to mind as you record your research. Fortunately, there are simple mechanical means to help you do this.

While construction, organization and development may be pleasant, they also can consume vast amounts of time. So it is important that you always keep efficiency in mind. Creativity, of course, demands some intellectual breathing-space, but you must be sure to distinguish between the necessary conditions for creative thought and mere dissipation of energy. As you write note-cards, make an outline, and write the first draft of your paper, verify that what you are doing and thinking are relevant to the work at hand. Distraction, although mentally refreshing, must be used with care. Too much will deter your progress.

You must be as ruthless as possible with your

time, especially during the first steps of organization and development. Be thorough, but do not get delayed by details that have no functional value. Record all relevant data in enough detail so that you will not have to return to the sources later. But always ask yourself exactly how you will use the information you are writing down. It is very frustrating to have to throw away half of your note-cards because there is no place for them in your paper.

Part of efficient organization and research is the quick dissection of the books and articles that form the basis of your paper. Do not feel obliged to consume such materials *en masse;* select only what you need. Skim the irrelevant and introdustory portions. Since even the most profound studies are surrounded with intellectual dead wood and literary procedures that have little ideational content, do not be disturbed when an article turns out to have little or nothing worth recording. Verify that you have done your best to extract meaningful ideas, and move on to the next source.

Bibliographical Notes

Record the bibliographical data of all books and articles as soon as you have decided to use them. Be very precise; rushing to the stacks of your library to verify a publication date as you type your final draft is needless torture. Use one three by five note-card to designate each of your sources. On that card record the author's name, the title of the reference, the place and date of publication, the call number of the book, and the page and chapter numbers of the parts that you intend to use. At the same time write down any other bibliographical information that should appear in your paper's citations.

This card will be the *master-card* for all quotations and thoughts that you take from a particular work. If you feel that you can save time by assigning a code number or letter to this card and using that symbol to designate all textual notes taken from the reference, do so. But remember that if you use such symbols, you cannot afford to misplace the master-cards without instantly transforming your careful research into a meaningless jumble of orphaned quotations.

By recording all bibliographical information when you have the original sources in front of you, you have composed your bibliography. All you need to do is to shuffle the cards into alphabetical order and type them on the last page of your paper.

Textual and Commentary Notes

When writing textual and commentary notes, you may decide not to use the symbol system to designate the work from which the note is drawn. If so, do not skimp on the bibliographic information that must appear at the top of each card. Write the author's last name in full, and abbreviate the title by using two or three full words rather than a condensed word for each full word of the title. The reason for such caution is that home-brewed abbreviations lose their meaning almost as soon as you think of them. For example, two weeks later, while you are typing your footnotes, there are few ways of knowing for sure that "Child & Sty" means *Childhood and Society*.

Supply yourself with plenty of three by five inch note-cards. Keep them directly beside the source you are reading so that you can instantaneously transcribe every piece of relevant information. Write a separate card for each distinct quotation or major idea so that you can shuffle them to build your paper's structure. Failure to take this fairly tedious step might force you to cut a single card into two or three strips in order to manipulate two or three different pieces of information later on. Do not waste time by recording inessential digressions; but do transcribe the potentially relevant sentence, even if it's only ten words long.

In addition to bibliographical symbol or information, every card should contain a page number, volume number when applicable, and any other useful reference data. You may write tentative headings for your note-cards if you are fairly sure of the shape of your paper, but it usually is safer to do this after you have completed some preliminary arrangement of notes and ideas.

Be as thorough and precise in recording ideas that arise while reading as you are in recording textual notes. Various paragraphs, sentences, and even footnotes in the source may trigger a profitable chain of thought, and it is essential that you are aware of such ideas. Complete records of the provocative ideas that come into your head while you read will prevent anguished searches when you come to write your outline and first draft. The fleeting thought is truly lost unless you write it down.

Organizing Notes

Once you have assembled all the data necessary to develop your thesis, stop taking textual notes and refuse to return to the sources unless you absolutely must. Now is the time to organize both your notes and your thoughts. Familiarize yourself with your note-cards. You may find that some kind of inherent order emerges after you have read them through three or four times. If not, begin to organize them by reduction. First divide your note-cards into a few general categories, then take each general category and break it down further. Continue this process until the shape of your paper is clear, but do not reduce so far that most categories contain only one or two cards. Simply divide your data into workable and meaningful groups. When you have done this, you may find that particular small groups in different general categories are closely related. If so, try to merge them to make your outline and first draft more coherent. Finally, write headings on every card in a particular group. This will prevent the destruction of all thematic order that comes when cards are removed from their separate stacks to be incorporated in your paper.

The Outline

While the impression of structure and development produced by categorizing note-cards is still fresh in your mind, write an outline. An outline is absolutely necessary for every paper. If you already know what your paper is going to look like, the outline will make sure that you do not forget; if you have no idea of your paper's final form, the outline will give you a chance to experiment with several structures before you must make a definite decision. An outline also will embody all the connections that you see between your note-cards and insure that your paper is proportioned according to the importance of your ideas, and not to the vagaries of your writing habits. Above all, an outline will preserve that intellectual thrust which you have been developing since you first began to think about an area of concern. Beware of squandering the possibility of excellence by failing to make an outline.

An outline can reduce the level of anxiety that accompanies the actual writing process. When you have organized your thoughts and references, foreshadowed your paper's introduction, development, and conclusion, and trimmed all irrelevant material by making an outline, you can be sure that the skeleton of your paper is complete. To flesh it out you need only follow the more detailed instructions of your outline. All the essentials are accounted for; you can spend the rest of your time writing rather than re-thinking.

Take care to write an outline that is more than a series of notes for the future. To insert parenthetical words like (expand) or (develop) is far from expanding or developing the idea at hand; it is only procrastination. Without going into unnecessary detail, try to indicate precisely and concretely how you will treat every idea that occurs in the outline. Finishing your paper without frantic labor is a more than sufficient reward for a painstaking outline.

The First Draft

A writer's block is no myth. For reasons unknown, the sight of an unblemished sheet of paper and a pen can paralyze even the most articulate people. They sit before that intimidating piece of paper, do nothing for hours, and gradually lose impetus. Any urge to write that they may have brought to the task evaporates completely; sometimes it never returns, and writing is accomplished because of deadline pressure alone. But this is a valuable lesson: it shows that writing is more a matter of will than of inspiration. If outside pressure successfully forces writing, then inside pressure can do the same. All it takes is determination.

The actual labor of writing is comparatively slight when you are working from a detailed outline and note-cards. It consists primarily of translating into prose the ideas that the outline expresses in shorthand. Like any translator, you will have to search for meaningful English equivalents of the material you are converting and supply transitional phrases or minor ideas that are not explicit. Fortunately, these tasks are accomplished without much thought once you actually begin to write.

There is only one way to build up the momentum that will carry you through the writing phase —start writing. Continue for at least three or four pages in order to conquer inertia. If you find that the words still refuse to flow with some ease, perhaps a short rest will help. But do not take anything more than a *short* rest—distraction is more a danger at the writing table than anywhere else. Despite any initial pain, you will find that writing comes more easily as you do more of it. For this reason you should not stop writing unless you absolutely must; it is foolish to conquer the first, most difficult hurdle, continue for a short while, and then stop, only to confront that same hurdle again. Take as much advantage of your flying start as you can.

Obviously, concerning yourself with matters of style and expressiveness at this point can undermine your writing. Forget about the finer points of writing and concentrate on putting across your ideas as best you can. Pay attention to the logical progression of your thought and avoid haphazard statements. Try to make sure that everything you say can be justified either by a reference or by the reasoning that has preceded it. Remember also that those who read your paper know nothing of the thinking and research that have gone into it, and your duty to yourself is to make sure that you say everything you want to say. Oversimplification and too elaborate explanation can make your paper seem tedious and naive; but they are less harmful than obscuring the background of your research and the connections among your ideas. In general, your arguments should begin to seem like inevitable conclusions naturally following from the facts.

When you have finished your first draft, forget about it for a little while. Relax and think about something else until you feel that your mind is clear and fresh enough to take an absolutely objective look at what you have done, or at least a new and unbiased look. Then sit down with your draft and a blue pencil. First read it over at medium speed, checking to be sure that you have included and connected all the major points of your thesis. Then go over your draft again, but very slowly. Work your way through line by line and paragraph by paragraph, ruthlessly dealing with fuzzy phrases, incomprehensible constructions, and awkward transitions. Strike out everything that detracts from your argument, that impedes the strong forward motion of ideas. Rewrite only when the defective segment is indispensable. You probably can eliminate the equivalent of several paragraphs without detracting anything from the real value of your work. When you must rewrite, simplify sentences and make them more forceful. Bleach purple prose to a more rational tint. Verify that each sentence is complete and that every pararaph coheres. Divide paragraphs that crowd too many ideas together and combine those that contain only a fragment of an idea. Take care not to mutilate the sense and development of your paper, but be as strict as you can. In the eyes of your reader, a paper that looks slapped together actually was composed that way.

After revising your draft, you need only type it in acceptable form and make minor alterations. Your term paper is almost completed.

CHAPTER 4

Structure and Form

THE best packages show the consumer exactly what they contain. They provide information about net weight, ingredients, and use, as well as a picture of the product. The same is true of the best term papers. They first tell the reader everything about the material that lies beyond the introduction—its relative length, major ideas, implications, and general shape. Thus the reader knows precisely what he is supposed to get, and he is suitably impressed when it is delivered as advertised. To begin your paper with a statement of the problem, its background, and your ways of dealing with it is both courteous and strategic. It makes understanding the paper much easier and prevents unnecessary confusion because of sudden, unexpected immersion in new ideas and arguments. But it also conveys an impression of complete control and trenchantly analytical thought.

Your paper should be divided into several definite sections. Generally, these should be an introduction, a presentation of the pertinent facts and arguments, and a conclusion. This structure can be varied, but its basic features always should be included. Sometimes it is best to emphasize one part of this structure more than usual. A survey paper, for example, might devote more time to background than to argument; an analysis of one methodological point, however, could afford to skimp on the background and stress argument instead. Variations in structure grow organically from the nature of the paper.

Moderate repetition at the beginning and end of a paper can help to further the impression of control and rationality. Stating what you intend to accomplish, accomplishing it, and summarizing the progression of your ideas is a very effective combination. It says simply that you have succeeded in what you intended to do, a statement so apparently incontrovertible that only the most captious critic will question whether what you set out to do was worth doing at all. Also, if you first state and justify the limitations of your work, you will avoid the trap of being criticized for failure to perform something you never offered to perform.

Proper footnotes and bibliography are essential both to the validity of a paper and to the impression of competence that it seeks to give. The format for these addenda is fairly standard.

Footnotes

The biggest question here is when to footnote and when not to. Fortunately, there are some generally accepted practices:

Do footnote statistics;
controversial facts or dates;
quotations;
other people's opinions and answers;
and special definitions or descriptions furnished by others.

Do not footnote the same information twice;
works already cited, when you men-

> tion the author in the body of the text; and
> a single work to which you can refer by placing the page number in parentheses after an excerpt.

If your paper uses only *Childhood and Society,* parenthetical page numbers will suffice; but if it also uses *Young Man Luther,* footnotes are required.

Most books supply footnotes at the bottom of the page on which they occur, for this allows the reader to make instant reference. Most doctoral dissertations follow the same practice, but less formal papers do not. Rather, they amalgamate all footnotes on separate footnote pages at the end of the paper. If you have very good reasons for being courteous to your reader and can organize the division of your pages into text and footnote sections, place your footnotes at the bottom of the page; but if your reader is not demanding and you are lazy, footnote pages will be adequate.

If the source you cite is a book, information should appear in the following order: name of the author (first name first), title of book, place of publication, publisher, date of publication, and page number. Other information—volume number, section number, etc.—should appear between the date of publication and the page number. Footnotes should be spaced singly and punctuated uniformly, and the first line of the footnote should be indented:

> Erik Erikson, *Insight and Responsibility* (New York: W. W. Norton, 1964), p. 69.

Note that the name of the author is followed by a

comma, the title of the book is underlined with no succeeding comma, publishing information appears in parentheses followed by a comma, place of publication is followed by a colon, and date of publication is separated from publisher by a comma.

Footnotes for periodicals are slightly different:

Curt Richter, "The Phenomenon of Unexplained Sudden Death in Animals and Man," *Journal of Genetic Psychology*, LXXIII (1948), p. 13

Note that the title of the article is in quotation marks and followed by a comma, the title of the periodical is underlined and followed by a comma, the volume number appears in Roman numerals, and the date is enclosed in parentheses and followed by a comma. Variations include:

1. If the article has no byline, author and title simply are eliminated and the form remains the same.

2. If an issue number appears, the volume number written in Roman numerals is followed by a comma, and the issue number, written in Arabic numerals, follows—e.g., IX, 8 (1970). If only the year or the month and year of publication are available, they appear without parentheses, and both of them are followed by commas—e.g., March, 1949.

After you have cited a book in full, you can use three devices to abbreviate footnotes:

1. If only one of the author's works is used, cite his last name, insert a comma, and give the page number of the reference.

2. If more than one book by the same author appears, write the name of the author, title of the book, and the page number.

3. If the footnote immediately preceeding cities the same author and work, use the abbreviation *Ibid.*, which is always underlined and followed by a comma and the page number.

Examples of these forms might include:

(1) Erikson, p. 87
(2) Erikson, *Identity, Youth, and Crisis*, p. 78
(3) *Ibid.*, p. 15

If you have used many types of sources, divide your bibliography into sections devoted to each type. Bibliographical form is identical to footnote form except for three points: the author's name appears with the last name first, a period replaces the comma after the author's name and appears after the title, and the parentheses are lifted from the publication data. Thus:

Erikson, Erik. *Insight and Responsibility.* New York: W. W. Norton, 1964.

CHAPTER 5

Style

PARADOXICALLY, style is ineffable. Although we can isolate some of its elements and describe some of its manifestations, we cannot say precisely what it is. In some ways, style is precision, the ability to say exactly what you mean. Thus it is connected with clear thinking, for precise expression of fuzzy thoughts is impossible. Yet clear thinking is not a sufficient condition for style. Perhaps the most useful description is that style makes a good paper readable and intelligible while lack of style or bad style renders that same paper difficult and needlessly obscure.

Style is integral to a good paper. It is not an ornament tacked on as an afterthought. Neither does it come between reader and writer, for it must foster clarity in all ways. Nor is style ever very prominent; if it is, then it is bad style.

Unfortunately, most academic papers are stylistically inferior or have no style at all. They suffer from jargon, unnecessary convolution, awkward constructions, and formalistic nonsense. Many demonstrate a remarkable insensitivity to language and an ignorance of everyday grammar. These are serious faults in papers that are supposed to spread knowledge.

Happily, you can avoid major stylistic blunders by adhering to a few general principles and specific rules. Most of them are summarized in Strunk and White's *The Elements of Style,* a brief, sensible map of writing's hazards. While we cannot hope to replace this classic in a few pages, we can adapt some of its principles for our own use.

The first principle is that you are writing in order to communicate and therefore should make sure that you do. Your goal is to make people understand your thought as well as linguistically possible. In short, the first principle is *clarity above all.*

Second, *write what comes naturally.* Write as you would speak when trying to make another person really understand you. This second principle is not a blanket pardon for destroying the English language; what it urges is that you shun formalisms, complications, and pedantries. Such elements cloud the reader's perception of your ideas. Besides, they make writing more difficult and unpleasant than it has to be.

Thirdly, *be concise and specific.* Examine each sentence to see whether you can compress it without mutilating its meaning. Remember that loose, rambling sentences tax the reader's attention span and dispel the force of your ideas. Short, powerful sentences are more effective. The same is true for specificity: vague words and clauses seldom impress anybody. Make the vague parts of your paper as concrete, as intellectually real as possible.

These three principles will do much to improve the style of your paper. But some smaller, specific points can do almost as much. Among the most important:

1. *Use nouns and verbs.* Not even the most powerful adverbs and adjectives can restore force to a sentence weak in nouns and verbs. Modifiers

often do no more than complicate a poor sentence.

2. When you have a choice, *use the active and not the passive voice.* The active voice naturally breathes more life into your writing than the limp passive does. "The concept of alienation was attacked by Allport" is but a bloodless version of "Allport attacked the concept of alienation."

3. *Avoid trite phrases, fancy words, and awkward constructions.* Few things weaken a sentence as surely as a phrase like "the grass is always greener," and attempts to formalize such clichés usually accentuate their inadequacy—"Not always is the grass so green . . ." Fancy words and awkward constructions debilitate sentences in similar ways.

If you observe the three principles and these three specific rules while editing your draft, the result will be so much cleaner and more comprehensible than the original that you may not recognize it. But your reader will recognize it as a superior paper.

CHAPTER 6

Term Paper Tips

DISTRESSINGLY enough, readers are prone to mark down papers for minor defects, few of which have any bearing on the real quality of the paper. And even when they limit evaluation to more substantive elements, they cannot fail to notice annoying details. If such defects are at all numerous, they can prejudice the most equitable reader.

Thus it is common sense to protect your investment of time and effort by doing all in your power to eliminate defects of appearance, form, and approach. You probably cannot cut out all of them, for each reader has idiosyncrasies beyond anyone's comprehension. But there are some small points that will annoy almost any reader. Fortunately, they are easy to avoid.

1. *Type neatly.* Some students err by turning in handwritten papers, and single spaced ones at that. This is a grave mistake, for it can make the reader's task inordinately difficult. Avoid it by typing your paper, and typing it neatly. Remember that corrections suggest hesitation, mistakes, and hurried composition.

2. *Proofread.* It is senseless to devalue your effort by refusing to spend twenty minutes checking your paper for errors of grammar, spelling, typing, and collation.

3. *Streamline.* Avoid the impression of disorganization and uncertainty made by superfluous

references, frequent repetitions, unpruned ideas, and dangling thoughts. Eliminate all marginal ideas; eliminate note-cards that do not make a concrete contribution to your paper.

4. *Take nothing for granted.* If you do, your reader may take it for granted that you do not really know what you are talking about.

5. *Subdivide.* Most papers over ten pages long become clearer to both writer and reader when they are divided and subdivided into sections that reflect the major structural parts. This simple step can clarify the main points of your paper more than seems possible at first.

PART II

TERM PAPER TOPICS

A Note on Using This Section

THE following pages offer a broad sampling of topics for papers in sociology. As the field itself is so broadly defined, we have included topics that range from the historical and interdisciplinary to the methodological. Almost every conceivable kind of topic between those extremes also appears. Rather than quibbling about the criteria of purely sociological concerns, we have selected these topics primarily on the bases of interest and potential for expansion and adaptation.

These topics were written to indicate the directions in which a good paper can go and to indicate what a useful topic-approach combination looks like. You are urged to use them as a taking off point for your own ideas rather than to write on them as they stand. Pay particular attention to the transformations that a simple change in approach or variation in idea can effect; you can adapt these topics to your unique needs in similar ways. As every topic can be approached in three or four ways and actually involves two or three component ideas, each of which can be altered slightly, the functional number of our suggestions for sociology papers is incalculable.

The topics are grouped into nine areas of concern, and the areas of concern are further grouped into four general classifications:

Group I—Social Structure
- The Origins of Society
- Social Structure and Institutions
- Social Change

Group II—Man in Society
- The Individual and Society
- Social Psychology and Group Interaction

Group III—Culture—Past and Present
- Society in Comparative and Historical Perspective
- The Origins, Structure and Process of Modern Society

Group IV—Meta-Sociology
- The Sociology of Knowledge
- Interdisciplinary, Philosophic, and Methodological Concerns of Sociology

The topics are rated for difficulty on a I to III scale in which I is the easiest and III the most difficult. Generally, a topic rated III differs from a topic rated I because it requires more research, more development, more background in the field, and more sustained analysis of a more difficult problem. But the ratings still are somewhat arbitrary; they represent only the opinions of those who wrote them, and not your own. So, do not be scared away from a topic because of its rating.

The sample topic below shows the typographical format for all topics. The first line, set in **bold face,** is the title of the topic. The second section, set in *italics,* details the central problems of the topic, while the third section, in regular roman typeface, discusses the approach to this problem. Finally, the fourth section, set in smaller type, indicates relevant references.

Alcoholism and Social Class

How is alcoholism a function of social class? What does information on the social and psychological sources of alcoholism imply about this relationship? How are these social and psychological factors interrelated?

Examine statistics on alcoholism for the past fifty years. If possible, compare urban alcoholism with rural. Show how these statistics relate to sociological studies of the variations in escapist behavior according to class.

Trice, *Alcoholism in America*
Cavan, *Liquor License*
Pittman and Snyder, *Society, Culture, and Drinking Patterns*

(II)

Social Structure

The Origins of Society

The Origins of Civilization

Sociologists have been able to contribute some valuable ideas to other disciplines about the origins of culture, primarily by analyzing different societies. How has such work supplemented or contradicted that of psychologists?

Use as an example Freud's theories of the origins of civilization and analyze the value of Malinowski's and Brown's criticisms of those theories. Ruth Benedict's remarks on the subject are a useful guide.

Freud, *Civilization and Its Discontents*
Malinowski, *Sex and Repression in Savage Society*
Brown, *Life Against Death*
Benedict, *Patterns of Culture*

(II)

Archetypes and Social Experience

The most basic elements of our experience often crystalize themselves in general symbols—arche-

types—that persist through centuries and across cultures. Many of these archetypes are rooted in the most fundamental structures of society—the family, social domination, and duty are examples.

Examine which of the most stable elements of the collective mind are the products of social interaction rather than of biology or economics. You will have to make some fine distinctions.

Campbell, "The Imprints of Experience," in *The Masks of God*, volume I
Jung, *Psyche and Symbol*
Eliade, *Myth and Reality* and *The Sacred and the Profane*

(II)

Early Community Life and Modern Civilization

"Neolithic" village community life seems to have been a prerequisite for higher civilizations everywhere. Using data from both the Old and the New World, discuss the social, economic, technological, religious, and political changes that accompanied and, in part, prepared the way for this early kind of life.

Compare several anthropological monographs on the subject. What factors seem to relate forms of interaction and community cohesion in different areas?

Clark, *Archeology and Society* and *World Pre-history: An Outline*
Gabel, *Analysis of Prehistoric Economic Patterns*

(I)

Urbanism: An Anthropological Analysis

Although urbanism is a relatively "recent invention," it did pose problems for prehistoric soci-

eties. What were these problems, and what sorts of solutions were found? How do present problems of urbanism compare with prehistoric ones?

Compare studies of contemporary urban societies and of the modern expansion of urbanism with monographs on prehistoric cultures. Base your comparison on at least three parallel functions of cultural survival.

MacGowan and Hester, *Early Man in the New World*
Wormington, *Ancient Man in North America*
Riesman, *The Lonely Crowd*

(I)

Man and His Gods

Social structure seems closely tied to structures of belief in the supernatural. Discuss the relationship between hierarchies and family structures in both realms and show how the existing social structure often is extended into the supernatural realm through ancestor worship and other means.

Analyze separately and diagram the social structure and the structure of the supernatural system in one particular tribe. Indicate their interrelationships and state whether they are limited or pervasive, central or peripheral in importance.

Wallace, *Religion: An Anthropological View*
Panikkar, *Hindu Society at the Crossroads*
Swanson, *Birth of the Gods*

(III)

Primate Ground Adaptation Patterns as Models of Proto-Human Behavior

Man first discovered his role on earth when he was forced to abandon the receding forests and take to the savanna. Some primate species are in the same position today. How much of a key to man's origins lies in different primate responses to a difficult environment?

Outline and discuss the adaptive behavior of the Patas monkey and the baboon as ground-dwelling species. Then relate these adaptations to the problems early man may have encountered and the solutions he may have found.

Pfeiffer, *The Emergence of Man*
Jay, *The Primates*
Ardrey, *African Genesis*

(II)

The Stages of Cultural Development

To aid broad comparisons, sociologists have described cultural development as a series of stages. If this description is valid, it should be possible to see similarities among cultures at the same general stage of development. Do such similarities exist? How might the "stage approach" be modified to make it relevant for comparing apparently dissimilar societies?

Describe similarities and differences in a stage comparison of two societies—either the New World Paleo-Indian and the Old World Paleolithic or the North American Archaic and the Northern European Mesolithic.

Thomas, *The Harmless People*
Clark, *World Prehistory: An Outline*
Leakey, *Stone Age Africa*

(III)

The Clark Model of Early Societies

Clark has proposed a tripartite scheme for the interrelationship of culture, habitat, and biome in a developing society. Do the relationships that actually exist conform to the Clark model? If not, how might the model be extended or altered to make it more valuable in investigating early cultures?

Compare at least three monographs on prehistoric cultures in the framework of the Clark model. Explore other theoretical models of prehistoric culture and attempt to synthesize them.

Clark, *Archeology and Society* and *World Prehistory: An Outline*
Howell and Bourliere, *African Ecology and Human Evolution*
Ardrey, *African Genesis*

(II)

An Exercise in Cultural Relativism

Members of a culture find it difficult to perceive their own subtle and pervasive ethnocentrism, but outsiders often understand it with ease. In trying to view your own culture as an outsider, what evidence of ethnocentrism can you see? Is the insider's blindness to this evidence functional or dysfunctional for his culture?

Choose and describe one major institution of your culture as though you were an anthropologist of the next century. Try to be as clinical as possible and pay special attention to correspondences between this institution and those of more primitive societies. Suggest whether and how ethnocentrism might be diminished.

Hall, *The Silent Language*

(I)

Family Structure of Apes and Humans

Animal behavior often is very relevant to human behavior, and the family structure of apes is particularly useful in trying to understand human family structure. What correspondences can you see? Do particular patterns of behavior carry over from primate family structure to the human version? If so, how much?

Describe the relevant patterns of behavior and, where there are no specific carry-overs, suggest how primate behavior in this sphere gives useful hints about the underlying structure of human families.

Lorenz, *On Aggression*
Reynolds, "Kinship and the Family in Monkeys, Apes, and Man," *Man*, June, 1968

(II)

Infant Dependency in Primates

Most primates experience an extraordinarily long period of nurturant dependence on their mothers. How is this extended dependency related to the complex learned behavior necessary to an advanced species' maintenance and survival? What does relationship suggest about the dependency period as a function of human development and socialization?

Compare at least three different species of primates. Pay special attention to elements of behavior that relate to the process of socialization —dominance and submission behavior, defensive behavior, and mating activities.

Jay, *The Primates*
Etkin, *Social Behavior from Fish to Man*
DeVore, *Primate Behavior*

(II)

Social Structure and Institutions

Political Parties Past and Present

In Western democracies, the evolution of external and internal strategies owes much to the evolution of political parties. How have such strategies been affected by changes in the social classes, ethnic groups, regions, and interest groups that make up the dominant parties? What are the perceptible effects of changing leadership, membership, and party machinery?

Library Research: analyze and interpret monographs dealing with parties at different periods of time; then try to relate party changes to the political and social history of those periods.

Neumann, *Modern Political Parties*
Roche, *Parties and Pressure Groups*
Duverger, *Political Parties*
Lipset, *Party Systems and Voter Alignments*
Michels, *Political Parties: the Oligarchical Tendencies of Modern Democracies*
Crotty, *Party Organization*

(III)

Freud and Weber on Religion and Society

Both Freud and Weber had definite, original ideas about the complex interrelationship between religion and society. Exactly how much importance do these thinkers attribute to religious ideology when viewing the structure, processes, and changes in society? What are their main points of difference?

Compare the views of Freud and Weber on the essential role of religion in society. Then detail their accounts of how religious ideology affects social psychology, art, politics, and other societal phenomena. Explain why one view seems more reasonable than the other.

Freud, *Moses and Monotheism* and *The Future of an Illusion*
Weber, *Sociology of Religion* and *Ancient Judaism*

(II)

The Political Sociology of Robert Michels

Michels wrote a classic work on the structure of political parties. Since his time, though, there have been many new and exciting contributions to the theory of political parties. How does Michels measure up against a modern theorist?

Choose one modern theorist and compare his work to that of Michels. Specific points of comparison might include the relationships of parties to pressure groups, types of party leadership, duties and rights of members, composition of membership, etc.

Michels, *Political Parties*
Lipset, *Political Man*

(II)

Tension and Balance in Resolving Social Conflict: The Indian Model

To survive, a culture must have an expedient social structure that provides stability and identity for its members while it reduces as much as possible the tensions of intergroup and interpersonal relationships. Discuss the Indian caste system in terms of its conflict-resolving functions.

Examine the social, economic, interpersonal, and religious functions and origins of the caste system. What specific needs does it fulfill? How successful is it? In what ways and for what reasons has it failed?

Blunt, *The Caste System of Northern India*
Dhurye, *Caste and Class in India*
Srinivas, *India's Villages*

(I)

The Necessity of Conflict

If social cohesion is a healthy state, then social conflict is a diseased one. Is the dichotomy that simple? Examine and compare the thoughts of sociologists who believe that these states are complements rather than opposites.

Compare the positions of Marx, Sorel, Simmel, and Dahrendorf on this point to determine whether social conflict actually is necessary to social cohesion, to what extent it is so, and whether another alternative is required in light of an emerging, larger society.

Marx, *Poverty of Philosophy*
Sorel, *Reflections on Violence*
Simmel, *Conflict* (especially pp. 13-17)
Coser, *The Functions of Social Conflict* (see pp. 151-156)
Dahrendorf, "Out of Utopia: Toward a Reorientation of Social Analysis," *American Journal of Sociology*, LXIV.

(II)

The Function and Ritual of Diplomacy

Many archaic ceremonies and rituals of diplomacy have survived to this day. Do they serve any real function in terms of statecraft?

Analyze the current ritual and ceremony of diplomacy. Determine whether they have relevant symbolic functions or whether they are irrelevant or even detrimental to the real business of diplomacy.

Ullman, "Education and Training for Our New Diplomacy," *Annals of the American Academy of Political and Social Science*, November, 1968

(I)

Status and Its Symbols

How does an individual in a particular position try to distinguish himself from individuals in other vocational positions? How do individuals of similar vocational status choose common symbols? What are the functions of these common symbols? In what ways are they dysfunctional for society?

Choose one status group—managers, for example—and point out the symbols that distinguish it. Include evidence like costume, flexibility of working hours, office arrangements, and eating habits. How do these symbols help or hinder the manager's functions?

Hughes, *Men and Their Work*
Merton, *Reference Groups and Social Structure* and *Social Theory and Social Structure*

(I)

The Family—Agent or Victim of Socialization?

In contemporary society agencies like schools and the mass media have encroached upon the family's traditional role as socializer of the individual. Is the family still a viable agent of socialization? How viable are the alternatives?

Library Research: examine monographs on traditional, rural families versus modern, urban families and studies of the abolition of families. Statistics on divorce rates, size of families, school age, etc. may support your conclusions.

Russell, *Marriage and Morals*
Moore, *Political Power and Social Theory*
Spiro, *Children of the Kibbutz*

(II)

Bureaucracy and Literature

What is the place of bureaucracy in the modern European novel? What does it tell us in general about the concerns of modern man? How have the societies that produced certain novels affected the authors' visions of bureaucracy?

Contrast Camus' and Kafka's characterizations of bureaucracy, paying special attention to their differing views on how bureaucracy manipulates man and the implications for human freedom. Then discuss Betti's play in this context. Determine how much the three writers feel that the problem of bureaucracy has its roots in the "nature of man."

Camus, *The Stranger*
Kafka, *The Trial* and *The Castle*
Betti, *Corruption in the Palace of the Justice*

(I)

Education—Creativity or Conformity?

The educational process often has been criticized for producing conformist attitudes and behavior. Should educators try to encourage creativity rather than conformity? If so, how might they go about it? What might be the long-range impact of such an educational approach on society?

Critically analyze the following writings. Decide whether any of them really offer positive alternatives to conformist education. Could a synthesis of these writings lead to a feasible system of creative education?

Read, *The Redemption of the Robot*
Leonard, *Education and Ecstasy*

(II)

The Dimensions of Class in Marxist Thought

Is the Marxist analysis of class sufficient to explain all social behavior? What elements does Marx take for granted that are hard to explain through "historical materialism"?

Consider examples of primordial group solidarity like that of the family. Examine them as alternative forces in motivating human behavior and then state whether Marxist theory excludes them as contradictory or makes provision for supplementary bases of explaining human behavior.

Tucker, *Marx's Concept of Man*
Fromm, *Marx's Concept of Man*
Mead, *Coming of Age in Samoa*

(III)

Social Order—Durkheim and Freud

Compare the concept of social order in the works of Durkheim and Freud. Pay attention to their different treatments of how the member of society relates to social control and of the "collective conscience." How do these treatments compare with Parsons' theory of the superego and social systems?

Freud, *Civilization and Its Discontents* and *Totem and Taboo*
Durkheim, *The Division of Labor in Society*
Parsons, *The Superego and the Theory of Social Systems*
Nisbet, *The Sociological Tradition*

(II)

Are Bureaucracies Inevitable?

Bureaucracies seem to be an inevitable part of modern political systems. Despite complaints about "red tape," social welfare and similar schemes would be impossible without a fairly elaborate organizational structure. Are there alternatives to bureaucracies that would accomplish necessary tasks without traditional drawbacks?

Examine how and why bureaucracies stifle individualism and the innovative impulses of society as a whole. Is bureaucratic behavior a universal phenomenon? How might it be altered? Does it vary with its goals?

Crozier, *The Bureaucratic Phenomenon*
Schumann, *Ideology and Organization in Communist China*
Argyris, *Personality and Organization*

(II)

Marxism and Elites

While Marxists genuinely believe in a popular revolution, they also recognize the need for a vanguard to lead the people. How can the question of elites be seen as a dilemma for Marxist thought? Has it ever been solved? If not, why? And what are the ramifications?

Discuss the role of elites in Marxist thought; how central is the idea to an understanding of Marx? Is it central to the coming of the revolution? How did Lenin's ideas about elites differ from Marx's?

Friedman, *Marxist Social Thought*
Bottomore, ed., *Karl Marx: Selected Writings on Sociology and Social Philosophy*
Lenin, *What Is To Be Done*

(II)

Mobility and Class Structure

In recent years, sociologists and historians have measured social mobility as a means of determining the relative fluidity of industrial society. Does social mobility really reflect social stratification? Why or why not?

Precisely how do studies of social mobility illuminate stratification in American society? Compare the findings of studies of social mobility with those of Mills. Basing your remarks on Thernstrom's *Poverty and Progress,* indicate how the study of mobility relates to orthodox Marxist theory.

Thernstrom, *Poverty and Progress*
Lipset, *Social Mobility in Industrial Society*
Sennett and Thernstrom, *Readings in Urban History*
Mills, *The Power Elite*

(III)

Power and Authority

According to Bierstedt, authority is status rather than an attribute of persons; therefore, authority is more institutionalized than power. Yet Weber stresses the personal dimensions of authority. Which view seems more reasonable? Is it possible to synthesize them?

Compare the theories of Weber and Bierstedt on authority and its relation to power. Determine which thinker most accurately analyzes the phenomenon of authority and its social or institutional status.

Weber, *From Max Weber: Essays in Sociology* (eds., Gerth and Mills), "Part II: Power"
Bierstedt, "An Analysis of Social Power," *American Sociological Review*, XV, number 6
Gerth and Mills, *Character and Social Structure*

(II)

Personality and Social Class

Is there a viable argument for a positive relation between social class and personality? Are there major scientific findings to support this hypothesis? What issues challenge its validity? How do the criteria used to measure personality affect the argument?

Examine current research on the interrelationship of personality and occupational structure. Use both analytical material in recent sociological monographs as well as analyses of personality.

Murphy, *Personality: A Bisocial Approach*
Yinger, *Toward a Field Theory of Behavior*
Cohen, *Social Structure and Personality: A Casebook*

(III)

Law in Society

Durkheim and Weber have very different views of the role of law in society. What are their positions? How do they correspond and conflict? Do essential differences in methodology underlie these differences of theory?

In comparing Durkheim's and Weber's views on this subject, pay special attention to their varying expositions of the relationship between the state and law. Determine how the state, as one expression of society, largely defines law, which is another.

Weber, *Economy and Society*
Durkheim, *The Division of Labor in Society*
Wolff, *Essays on Sociology and Philosophy*

(III)

The Meaning of Marriage

Homeostatic institutions tell a great deal about a society. How do Tikopian and Nuer marital relationships exemplify and comment on their respective societies? How might you rationalize the specific differences between these societies in terms of institutions, technologies, and physical environments?

Base your discussion on the factual information that appears in monographs. Be sure to consider the transactions that accompany the establishment of marriage, the division of labor between spouses, and the causes and frequency of divorce.

Evans-Pritchard, *The Nuer*
Firth, *We, The Tikopia*
Shapiro, *Human Society*

(II)

Social Class in the Thought of Marx and Weber

Marx and Weber had radically different views of the origin, functions, and the future of social class. What are their differences and similarities? How do their differences reflect their deeper theoretical divergences?

Compare the concepts of social class that appear in the *Communist Manifesto* and in *Economy and*

Society. Try to reconcile Marx's view of social conflict as external and inevitable with Weber's contention that such conflict is occasional and relatively unimportant.

Marx and Engels, *The Communist Manifesto*
Weber, *Economy and Society*
Lefebvre, *The Sociology of Karl Marx*
Freund, *The Sociology of Max Weber*
Zeitling, *Ideology and the Development of Sociological Theory*

(II)

Money in Simmel and Marx

How do Simmel and Marx approach the concept of money? How do they place it in the context of their systems of social analysis? How crucial is the concept of money to their theories?

Analyze Simmel's and Marx's views on money and compare their content, methodology, and relevance to each man's theories.

Simmel, *Essays in Sociology, Philosophy, and Aesthetics*
Wolff, ed., *The Sociology of Georg Simmel*
Marcuse, *Reason and Revolution*
Bottomore, ed., *Karl Marx: Selected Writings on Sociology and Social Philosophy*

(II)

Social Change

Misery and Rebellion

Is misery a helpful category in explaining social rebellion? Does the term have any real and/or behavioral meaning, or is it too vague and all-encompassing?

Critically examine explanations of rebellion and the terms they use. Decide whether these terms are too stereotypical to be both clear and helpful. State whether they account for rebellion satisfactorily.

de Tocqueville, *The Ancient Regime*
Tawney, *Agrarian Problems in the Sixteenth Century*
Hobsbawm, *Primitive Rebels*

(II)

Agents of Revolutionary Change

The causes of revolutionary change, a markedly complex phenomenon, may lie at different levels of experience: immediate pressures, long-term suffering, cultural anxiety, technological needs that demand a restructured society, etc. Which of these causes seems most to affect revolutionary change? How?

Concentrate on factors of class. Show how a differing array of the causes mentioned above moves different classes to revolt. Specifically, determine whether the declining pre-industrial lower class or the rising industrial proletariat has been the most radical agent of revolutionary change, and explain why.

Engels, *Revolution and Counter Revolution in Germany*
Hamerow, *Restoration, Revolution, and Reaction*
Moore, *The Social Origins of Dictatorship and Democracy*

(II)

Community and Social Mobility

Education is recognized as a key factor in social mobility. But is its effect entirely positive? How does education affect the community among de-

prived minority groups? Does upward mobility inevitably destroy that community?

Discuss arguments for and against preservation of the community in the face of such disintegrative forces. Determine whether new values can keep the community alive or whether the whole process of education and mobility so destroys traditional cultural bonds that survival is impossible.

Parsons and Clark, ed., *The Negro American*
Glazer and Moynihan, *Beyond the Melting Pot*

(III)

Will the Family Survive?

The contemporary family is a shaky institution: torn between vocational, household, and marital obligations, parents often cannot respond adequately to the social and psychological needs of their children. What is the future of the family? How might the conflicting obligations that threaten it be reconciled?

Consider the possibility of an alternative: a child-rearing institution and a part-time family. Decide if this is both a reasonable and a necessary development. Explore margins for improving the family in the post-industrial context.

Moore, *Political Power and Social Theory*
Russell, *Marriage and Morals*
Mace, *Marriage East and West*

(II)

The Printed Word and Social Interaction

The invention of printing influenced technology, intellectual life, and social relations. Exactly how did the serial combination of standardized char-

acters to compose words influence our ways of thinking about order and self-expression? How did this rethinking affect social interaction?

Describe the general cultural effects of Gutenberg's invention. After thoroughly examining Mumford's and McLuhan's works, critically compare them.

Mumford, *Art and Technics* and *Technics and Civilization*
McLuhan, *Understanding Media* and *The Gutenberg Galaxy*

(II)

The Family and Social Change

As an agent of socialization, as a primary group in general, and as an economic unit, the family is tied closely to the larger society. How and why do changes in that society affect the family's function and status? How, if at all, does the family itself affect the larger society?

Analyze the events in your own family over three or four generations. Talk to your relatives, their friends, and other interested parties in order to collect data on jobs held during particular years, political and economic experiences like the Depression and their personal effects, schooling, religion, clubs, reading, and housing. Notice closeness among certain relatives, hostility among others, and similar phenomena. When you have tabulated and summarized these data, relate them to historical events and political and economic trends in the larger society.

Myrdal, *Nation and Family*
Coser, *The Family, Its Structure and Functions*

(III)

New Patterns of Interaction in Young Socialist Countries

In Cuba and in China, Socialism attempts both material and social transformations. What new patterns of economic and social behavior do the leaders of the Cuban and the Chinese revolutions hope to develop? How necessary and close are the connections between these two kinds of change?

Describe these new patterns, both as ideals and as realities. Look for counterparts in other political and social systems. Evaluate and explain the possibilities of bringing the real patterns closer to the ideal.

Castro, *Why I Am a Marxist-Leninist*
Guevara, *Socialism* and *Man in Cuba*
Mao Tse Tung, *On Practice* and *On Contradiction*

(II)

Industrialization and Social Change

Industrialization and urbanization were accompanied by some of the most fundamental social changes experienced in man's history. What were these changes? How are they best described?

Compare the characterizations of these changes that appear in the works cited below. Discuss Mill's definition of the basic change in class structure and how that change affected the worker's consciousness and relation to his work. Compare the validity of the different characterizations of industrial and pre-industrial society. Finally, discuss whether these works were the results of objective research or of some preconceived ideological schema.

Mills, *White Collar: The American Middle Classes*
Polanyi, *The Great Transformation*
Lynd, *Middletown*
Sjoberg, *The Pre-industrial City*

(III)

The Social Bases of Revolutionary Groups

How does the social base of a revolution relate to its success? Which groups typically have supported revolutions, and which have fought them? Why and how have these different groups succeeded?

Compare the social bases of the French, American, Russian, and Cuban revolutions. Note common elements in their social bases and in those of the opposition. Suggest a theory to relate revolution and social groups.

Hobsbawm, *Social Bandits and Primitive Rebels*
Rude, *The Crowd in History*
Moore, *The Social Origins of Dictatorship and Democracy*
Guevara, *Man in Cuba*

(II)

Commercial Proprietors and Neighborhood Change

Property ownership can produce insight into the development and future of a neighborhood's social fabric. What can you deduce from an analysis of ownership? Does the analysis have implications for the stability or dynamism of the larger social environment?

Choose one block in a particular neighborhood, go into all the commercial establishments on that block, and collect data on the future, present, and past proprietors. Examine community records of ownership if available.

Thernstrom and Sennett, *Nineteenth Century Cities*
Fogel, *Qualitative Methods of Historical Analysis*

(III)

Changing Patterns in Education

Educational institutions are a major agent of socialization, and changes in them will have profound effects on society. Are such changes caused by outside pressure (from the public, the administration, etc.) or by internal, presumably evolutionary forces? In what ways do these changes affect society? Is there a feed-back loop in this case—i.e., *do changes in education genuinely change those forces or agents that urged change in the first place?*

Analyze past and present descriptions and prescriptions of education. Use educational journals and first-hand descriptions of school practice.

Paulsen, *Contemporary Issues in American Education*
Gross, *Radical School Reform*

(III)

Mobility and Meaningful Action

"Some of the major political problems facing contemporary society are, in part, a consequence of the conflict and tensions resulting from the contradictions inherent in the need for both aristocracy and equality." How valid is this thesis? What are its implications for meaningful political action?

Describe these tensions and show how they can be resolved when social mobility seems inevitable.

Determine whether politics can be a socially meaningful activity in a fluid, self-contradictory society that does not provide a coherent and consistent context for political action.

Lipset and Zetterberg, "A Theory of Social Mobility," *Transactions of the Third World Congress of Sociology*

Parsons, "A Revised Analytical Approach to the Theory of Stratification," in *Class, Status, and Power* (eds. Bendix and Lipset)

Tumin, "Some Principles of Stratification, a Critical Analysis," *American Sociological Review*

(III)

Man in Society

The Individual and Society

Family Status and Socialization

An axiom in the study of social structure is that cultural values transmitted to children depend on the status of the parents, and that the socialization of children invariably is oriented toward the future. How can you resolve this apparent paradox between the influence of the past and that of the future? Can you construct a role model for socialization that is neither static nor unrealistically mobile? How can such a model increase understanding of socialization?

Compare family systems in several very different cultures. Consider anthropological studies of primitive and/or developing cultures as well as sociological analyses of contemporary family systems.

Barber, *Social Stratification: A Comparative Analysis of Structure and Process*
Kluckholn, ed., *Personality in Nature, Society, and Culture*
Frazier, *Negro Youth at the Crossways: Their Personality Development in the Middle States*

(II)

The Stranger and Group Self-Concept

Both Schuetz and Simmel are concerned with the revelations that result from a stranger's confrontation with a group, particularly revelations concerning the self-concept of both entities. How valid are the contentions of both Schuetz and Simmel that the stranger is viewed as a type and that he offers objective criticism of the group?

Test these hypotheses by designing a questionnaire and distributing it to members of two kinds of communities—one that often confronts strangers and another that is insular by choice or circumstance. Design the questionnaire to bring out the group's ideas about its own identity, its relative moral and social structures, its values, and its characteristic relationships with outsiders.

Simmel, *The Sociology of Georg Simmel* (ed. Wolff)
Schuetz, "The Stranger, an Essay in Social Psychology," *American Journal of Sociology*, XLIX (1944)

(II)

Common Factors of Deviance

Both suicide and juvenile delinquency raise theoretical and methodological questions about the development of the individual and his interactions with society. Are these issues relevant to both suicide and delinquency in similar ways? Or are there major differences in the kinds of development and interaction that contribute to suicide and delinquency?

State the problem in general terms. Examine studies of suicide and delinquency to suggest a solution. Be sure to discuss how the methodological factors of the studies you use can affect the theoretical outcome.

Gibbs and Martin, *Status Integration and Suicide*
Matza, *Delinquency and Drift*
Clinard, *Sociology of Deviant Behavior*

(II)

The Child's Concept of Justice

How "innate" is the child's conception of justice? How much does family structure convey this concept, and how does social class determine it?

Visit kindergartens and playgrounds in neighborhoods of markedly different class characteristics. Try to approximate conceptions of fairness by observing play, argument, establishment of rules, etc. Note strong similarities, differences that might be caused by class background, and how a comparison of similarities and differences can lead to a concept of "innate" ideas of justice. Compare your findings to those of Piaget, who fails to account for class differences.

Piaget, *The Moral Development of the Child*

(I)

Alcoholism and Social Class

How is alcoholism a function of social class? What does information on the social and psychological sources of alcoholism imply about this relationship? How are the social and psychological factors interrelated?

Examine statistics on alcoholism for the past fifty years. If possible, compare urban alcoholism with rural. Show how these statistics relate to sociological studies of variations in escapist behavior according to class.

Trice, *Alcoholism in America*
Cavan, *Liquor License*
Pittman and Snyder, *Society, Culture, and Drinking Patterns*

(II)

The Social Function of Crime

Although destructive to the individual involved, crime often performs positive services for society at large. What are these services? How much do they justify accepting a certain level of crime as both necessary and beneficial?

Examine the thesis of socially useful crime in light of its obvious moral and physical disadvantages. Distinguish between the social utility of crime *per se* and that of punishment for crime. Suggest how the very possibility of crime serves to reinforce a culture's self-concept and self-assurance.

Durkheim, *The Rules of Sociological Method* (especially pp. 65-75)
Mead, "The Psychology of Punitive Justice," *American Journal of Sociology*, March, 1918

(III)

Character Formation and Social Process

Social theorists have attempted to account for character formation by using different, exclusive explanations based on psychology, ideology, or economics. Yet Fromm contends that character results from the individual's interaction with the social process, to which all of the factors listed above contribute. Is an exclusive explanation necessary or reasonable? Or is Fromm's thesis more than a way of dismissing the real factor(s) of character formation?

Consider alternative explanations of character formation and try to test all of the theses, including Fromm's, by analyzing character formation in your own family.

Fromm, *Escape from Freedom*
Erikson, "Identity and the Life Cycle," *Psychological Issues*, volume 1, number 1, 1959
Erikson, *Childhood and Society*
Fromm, *Marx's Conception of Man*

(II)

The Deviant and His Audience

To lead his whole life as a deviant, the individual must have an obvious and responsive audience. Exactly how does a society or subculture condone or reinforce deviant patterns? How do the role expectations of his audience affect the deviant and his career?

Examine first-hand accounts of deviant behavior to determine both social and economic reinforcements of deviance in the larger society. Detail the effects of role expectations and examine the particular problems of breaking out of the deviant mold.

Goffman, *Stigma*
Orwell, *Down and Out in Paris and London*
Sutherland, *The Professional Thief*

(I)

Alienation in Contemporary Society

"Alienation" is a particularly fashionable term used in many contexts, one of which is existential psychology and philosophy. How does alienation determine the content and approach of existential psychology and philosophy? What is the special meaning of alienation in this context? Does it have radically different meanings for psychology and philosophy?

Compare Marx's original use of the term with the ways that existentialists use it. Show how alienation is coterminous with industrialization and determine whether its existentialist meanings are more purely psychological (and "imaginary") than sociological (and "realistic"). Suggest how changes in the meaning and use of alienation reflect changes in the direction of social thought.

Josephson, *Man Alone*
Kaufmann, *Existentialism from Dostoevsky to Sartre*
Marx, *Economic and Philosophical Manuscripts*
Kenniston, *The Uncommitted*

(III)

Synanon—The Rehabilitation Game

A recent analysis suggests that Synanon, the drug addict rehabilitation organization, admits criminal addicts—people characterized by strong negative and rebellious attitudes toward society—and resocializes them to become ultra-conventional, "normal," self-reliant human beings. Is this analysis fair? What are the moral and ethical implications of a program of rehabilitation like Synanon's?

Study Synanon as well as other programs of rehabilitation. Pay special attention to the mechanisms that each of them uses to re-educate its population and to the assumptions that each of them makes about the dimensions and values of personal growth.

Yablonsky, *Synanon: The Tunnel Back*
Sussman, *Sociology and Rehabilitation*
Lindenfield, *Radical Perspectives on Social Problems*

(II)

Society and the Formation of the Self

Sociologists and psychologists have radically different opinions about the role that society plays in the formation of the self. What are the most striking differences between the sociological and the psychological position? Are these differences real, or only semantic confusions? Which view seems most valid?

Show how society influences the way in which the self is born. Detail arguments that show how the self is determined by one's social reality. Indicate how Goffman's, Freud's, and Royce's views differ, and attempt to synthesize them if possible.

Royce, *The Individual and Society*
Goffman, *Presentation of the Self in Everyday Life*
Mead, *Social Psychology*
Freud, *General Introduction to Psychoanalysis* and *The Ego and the Id*

(II)

Homosexuality and Social Integration

A recent study of homosexuality concludes that all deviants really subscribe to the larger society's values and at some level consider their deviance immoral. Covert homosexuals, for example, shun the company of overt deviants, and homosexuals who have children do not want their sons to become homosexuals. How do these findings fit in with recent theories of homosexuality and social deviance? Is the behavior that some sociologists take to indicate perceptions of immorality really a matter of survival?

Consider the focal concerns of the lower class and theories of subcultures, drift, and deviance as a boundary-maintaining process. Investigate several studies of homosexuality and compare their conclusions with your own theories.

Corey, *The Homosexual in America*
Schofield, *Sociological Aspects of Homosexuality*
West, *Homosexuality*

(II)

Social Reactions to Suicide

Statistical analyses often tend to ignore the larger relevance of the suicidal act, and individual case studies usually include little analysis of the social context of suicide. What are the characteristic social reactions to suicide and suicidal themes? Are these reactions specific for Western society, or do they hold true cross-culturally?

Examine studies of deviant behavior as well as specific analyses of the meaning of suicide. Consider how the mass media present suicidal themes.

Douglas, *The Social Meaning of Suicide*
Dublin, *Suicide*
Gibbs and Martin, *Status Integration and Suicide*

(II)

Identity Transformation in Institutions

What are the mechanisms that ensure a newcomer's total commitment to various highly or-

ganized institutions? What are the functions of initiation rituals, and why are they so frequently degrading? Do these mechanisms vary specifically with variance in the type of institution?

Analyze and compare studies of identity transformation. Concentrate on their similarities and give special reasons for differences. Specify the circumstances under which peer groups play central roles in identity transformation.

Goffman, *Asylums*
Lifton, *Thought Reform and the Psychology of Totalism*
Vidich and Stein, "The Dissolved Identity in Military Life," in *Identity and Anxiety* (eds. Stein, Vidich, and White)
Yablonsky, *Synanon: The Tunnel Back*

(II)

Rule-breaking Behavior

What level(s) of psychological, sociological, or biological analysis are most appropriate to explaining rule-breaking behavior? Is a moral, amoral, or super-moral concept of man relevant to discussions of rule-breaking?

Consider differential law-enforcement, the effects and definition of stigma, and the mechanisms that maintain deviant activity. Present your analysis in the framework of a developmental theory of the origin of rule-breaking behavior patterns.

Lemert, *Social Pathology*
Clinard, *Sociology of Deviant Behavior*
Lanais, *Current Perspectives on Social Problems*

(II)

Deviance and Confession

Sociologists disagree about the utility of confessional sessions as a means of rehabilitating devi-

ants. Organizations like Alcoholics Anonymous, Synanon, and Daytop Village, however, have institutionalized the confessional session as an integral part of their programs. How effective are such therapeutic measures? How do they compare with more punitive approaches? In what situations are confessional programs more effective than traditional methods of rehabilitation?

Pay particular attention to the ways in which both institutions and critical sociologists define "recovery" and "remission." Examine the conflict between the underlying principles of the confessional and the punitive methods of rehabilitation.

Erikson, *Wayward Puritans*
Johnson, *Crime, Correction, and Society*
Lindenfield, *Radical Perspectives on Social Problems*

(I)

White Collar Crime

Discussions of social deviance rarely emphasize "white collar crime" as much as other forms of deviant behavior. Why is this so? How does white collar crime resemble and differ from more traditional kinds of crime? Is it possible to analyze white colar crime as deviant behavior?

Discuss the meaning of society's reactions and the individual's feelings toward white collar crime and other types. Examine the effectiveness of legal sanctions for both kinds of crime. If possible, design and administer a questionnaire on attitudes toward white collar crime and other kinds.

Geis, *White Collar Crime*

Rubington and Weinberg, *Deviance: The Interactionist Perspective*
Becker, *The Other Side*

(II)

Anomie and Non-conformity

Anomie involves the absence of guides for social behavior and often creates a dilemma by providing the context for unlimited goals and means to achieve them. How does the illegitimate means to achieve these goals force the individual to violate accepted (but usually weak) social norms?

Suggest the ultimate consequences of anomie and of non-conformity. Discuss the price that the "free" individual must pay for violating strict, well-defined, and consistent social patterns.

Durkheim, *Suicide*
Merton, "Social Structure and Anomie," in *Social Theory and Social Structure*
Parsons, *The Social System*
Cloward, "Illegitimate Means, Anomie, and Deviant Behavior," *American Sociological Review*, XXIV, April, 1959

(III)

Man As a Social Animal

Sociologists continually point out that man is a highly socialized creature who internalizes social control from the very first moment of life. Wrong challenges this view by stressing what sociologists tend to neglect—man's bodily humiliation as a factor of control. How valid is Wrong's more comprehensive view? Are there any effective counter arguments? If not, can you propose some?

Discuss the extent of man's socialization. Decide whether the internalization of social control has been complete or whether it always come into conflict with man's organic nature.

Freud, *Civilization and Its Discontents*
Piaget, *The Moral Judgment of the Child*
Mead, *Mind, Self, and Society*
Durkheim, *Sociology and Philosophy*
Wrong, "The Oversocialized Conception of Man in Modern Sociology," *The American Sociological Review*, XXVI, pps. 184-193

(II)

Deviance and Control

Social scientists have suggested that methods of controlling deviance may be instrumental in maintaining the deviant behavior of various subcultures. Under what conditions do organized attempts to control deviance seem to have the opposite effect of encouraging it? What criteria can be used to distinguish those types of deviance that the authorities should ignore and those types that should be legally controlled?

Compare statistics on homosexuality, drug addiction, alcoholism, and other forms of deviant behavior in the United States with comparable statistics from Great Britain. Then try to indicate how change in law relates to changes in the occurrence of deviant activity.

Becker, *The Other Side*
Schur, *Crimes Without Victims*
Erikson, *Wayward Puritans*

(II)

Bureaucracy and Personality

Bureaucracy tends to include a special type of personality and to reinforce that type through promotion while it discourages nonconformity.

What is the impact of bureaucracy on the formation of personality?

Discuss bureaucracy's effects on the employee's role playing. Specify sanctions used to exclude personalities that do not fit in with the system. Determine the extent to which bureaucracy permanently influences the lives of employees.

Merton, *Social Theory and Social Structure*
Horney, *The Neurotic Personality of Our Time*
Argyris, *Personality and Organization*

(III)

Alienation and the Modern System

Despite sociologists' different concepts and uses of "alienation," one recurrent explanation for the phenomenon predominates: man is no longer alienated by his working conditions alone, but by the entire socio-economic fabric of society. What is the relative importance of the various causes of alienation?

In discussing these causes, decide whether a change in work conditions alone could relieve much alienation or whether a drastic revision of society as a whole is necessary to make men feel socially relevant again.

Blauner, *Alienation and Freedom*
von Pappenheim, *The Alienation of Modern Man*
Taviss, "Changes in the Form of Alienation: the 1900's versus the 1950's," *American Sociological Review*, February, 1969

(II)

Nurturance and Societal Roles

Social scientists have proposed several theories that relate specific forms of (culturally-defined) nurturance during childhood to specific types of role behavior among the mature members of a society. In analyzing this relationship among different cultures, can you see exactly which essential elements of nurturant behavior directly influence the formation of adult interactive and interpersonal styles? How is this influence transmitted?

Use monographs on child-rearing and nurturant behavior. In defining the characteristic styles of adults that relate to early experience, concentrate on aggression, mobility, and communication.

Erikson, *Childhood and Society*
Bowlby, *Maternal Care and Mental Health*
Kluckholn, ed., *Personality in Nature, Society, and Culture*

(II)

Feral Children—Myth and Experiment

Children reared by animals have been the subject of much creative literature. But psychologists also have focused on this phenomenon to determine how the individual is socialized, at what point of the life cycle socialization is possible, how the individual's capacity for symbolic behavior is actualized, and how the child learns language and other forms of symbolic interaction. How well and in what ways does creative literature on this subject accord with the findings of psychology?

In comparing such accounts, be sure to allow for and describe differences in the social backgrounds of the authors. Concentrate on the specific answers that each form of literature supplies to the question of the particular forms that socialization takes during childhood.

Hard, *The Wild Boy of Aveyron*
Campbell, "Wolf Children of India," *American Journal of Psychology*, number 38 (1927), p. 313 *ff*.
Kipling, *Mowgli, The Jungle Boy*

(II)

Social Psychology and Group Interaction

The Transitional Object Relationship

The developing infant forms "transitional" relationships with inanimate objects like teddy bears, onto which he projects a personality based on his own unfulfilled needs and desires. Psychologists find that this immature relationship in many ways resembles the adolescent love relationship. In what ways are they similar? What social needs does a transitional relationship satisfy? What are its limitations on an individual and on a social level?

Compare studies of infant development and behavior with psychological studies of the personality dynamics of adolescence. Critically analyze an interpersonal relationship of your own to see how the model of transitional object relationships applies. Indicate how specific societal demands influence the nature of an individual's interpersonal relationships.

Modell, *Object Love and Reality*
Erikson, *Childhood and Society*
Kagan, *Child Development*

(II)

Suicide and Homicide—A Racial Analysis

Sociological data confirm that whites generally have higher suicide rates than blacks, while blacks have higher homicide rates than whites. What are the implications of these facts in terms of social, economic, and class structures within both racial contexts?

Consider the sources of the statistics—whether they come from rural or urban areas, and what this means. Examine studies of the sources and motivations of suicide and homicide, particularly the social pressures that characterize areas and types of people with markedly high or low rates.

Rushing, *Deviant Behavior and Social Process*
Henry and Short, *Suicide and Homicide*
Wolfgang, *Studies in Homicide*

(II)

Attitudes Toward Tragedy

At certain times, tragic drama has been attacked as harmful to society; at others, it has been praised as a form of social and moral education, and something like group therapy. What explanations have been offered for both the detrimental and the beneficial effects of tragedy? What are the social dynamics of tragedy that appeal to certain writers?

Examine the writings of Aristotle, Tertullian, and Dryden. Can their differences of opinion be attributed mostly to the social conditions of their environment or to the ideology of their times? Evaluate the social justifications of tragedy that they offer.

Tertullian, *De Spectacularis*
Dryden, *Essay on Dramatic Poesie*
Aristotle, *Poetics*

(II)

Religion and Mental Illness

Religion is supposed to shape many of man's activities—socialization, vocation, etc. Mental illness often depends on variables of such activities and therefore may be influenced by religion. Can you establish valid connections between religion and mental illness?

Choose a published case of mental illness that seems to show the impact of religion, and base your analysis of it on theories presented in the references cited below. Try to correlate certain symptoms of the illness with certain religious experiences and influences that affected the individual.

Oates, *Religious Factors in Mental Illness*
Freud, *The Future of an Illusion*
Rokeach, *The Three Christs of Ypsilanti*

(II)

Leadership

Leadership can be viewed as both a psychological and a political phenomenon. What sorts of individuals become political leaders? How do their personal experiences, especially during adolescence, influence their modes of behavior as leaders? How does the leader's personality affect the impact he has on his followers?

Compare Martin Luther and Malcolm X as leadership personalities. Try to isolate common personality factors and show how they influenced both the rise to power and the later behavior of these two men. Pay special attention to sudden conversions and the advent of inspiration.

Malcolm X, *The Autobiography of Malcolm X*
Erikson, *Young Man Luther*

(I)

The Meaning of Sanity

The pressures of contemporary society—bureaucracy, ecological disaster, overcrowding, regulation of behavior by time and space—have forced many people into aberrant behavior, or madness, according to a simple psychological definition. Exactly how have these societal and environmental forces bred madness? And is the kind of behavior necessary to adapt to these conditions really sane?

Consider examples of the clinically insane to determine the influence of environmental factors. Decide whether the concept of insanity is meaningful in a society like ours or whether it dismisses rather than grapples with the problems of contemporary existence.

Laing, *The Divided Self*
Wolfe, *The Tangerine Flake Streamlined Kandy-Kolored Baby*
Spiro, *Children of the Kibbutz*
Stein, *Identity and Anxiety*

(III)

The Suicide Threat

Many people tend to discount suicide threats as hollow, but social psychologists feel that every threat should be taken seriously. Why is this so? How often is the threat realized, and under what conditions? If there are serious threats and hollow ones, how can they be distinguished?

Explain what a suicide threat really means in

socio-psychological terms. Describe how the "lethality" of threats can be measured, and indicate a general method for dealing with such threats. Use established procedures of Suicide Prevention Centers to illustrate your discussion.

Faberow and Shneidman, eds., *The Cry for Help* (especially chapters 2, 5, and 10) and *Clues to Suicide* (chapters 16 and 18)

Center for Studies of Suicide Prevention, National Institute of Mental Health, *Verbatim Transcript of Training Record in Suicidology*

(II)

A Psycho-Sociological Analysis of Witchcraft

Various sociologists have theorized that witchcraft is a method of social control, but psychologists suggest that witchcraft is an outlet for aggression and anxiety. Which position has more social, historical, and psychological validity? Or, if they are most valid when combined, how do these positions inter-relate?

Examine both historical and psychological studies of witchcraft. Look especially for evidence that suggests ways in which the one theory complements the other.

Huxley, *The Devils of London*
Warner, *A Black Civilization*
Douglas, *Purity and Danger*

(II)

Growing Up Through the Game

Mead, Campbell, and others have pointed out that the child matures as a symbolic animal by playing and that he begins to develop a socially organized personality through the game. How valid is this thesis?

Choose a simple and universal children's game like hide and seek and analyze the patterns of social interaction, cooperation, planning, and leadership that it incorporates and teaches to its participants.

Mead, *Mind, Self, and Society*
Huizinga, *Homo Ludens*

(II)

Schizoid Style—Aberration or Adaptation?

Many psychiatrists view schizoid behavior as an adaptation perfectly consistent with the demands of a certain environment. What kind of social environment leads to the development of schizoid style? What adaptive modes within the family or sub-culture characterize later schizoid behavior?

Review studies of the families of schizophrenics; examine objective case studies as well as the writings of schizoids themselves. Consider how both the immediate and the larger social environment make conflicting demands on the individual's adaptive capacities.

Henry, *Culture Against Man*
Esterman and Laing, *Sanity, Madness, and the Family*
Kaplan, *The Inner World of Mental Illness*

(III)

Normal vs. Abnormal—A Sociological Analysis

The criteria used to distinguish the normal from the abnormal often depend on the role expectations of a particular social environment. This is especially true for forms of sexual behavior. How normal or abnormal, in as absolute a sense as possible, are sexual patterns usually labeled deviant?

Focus at least part of your discussion on [illegible] sexuality and include cross-cultural reference[illegible] Moslem-countries and Classical Greece. Then pla[illegible] the issue within the context of social and clinica[illegible] definitions of character disorder.

Adams, "Mental Illness or Interpersonal Behavior?", *American Psychologist*, volume 19, number 3, 1964
Schofield, *Sociological Aspects of Homosexuality*
Goffman, *Interaction Ritual*

(I)

The Collective Superego in Crisis

Rapid social change, increasing awareness of cultural relativism, and mass society have caused the deterioration of the collective superego. What is the evidence of this deterioration? What were the dynamics of its development? Does it portend total death of the superego or a transition to a different kind of inner authority?

Consider Walter's article in the light of the other theories listed below. Determine whether and how these authors complement each other in their attempts to interpret or suggest a remedy for the absence of a superego in our culture.

Walter, "The Politics of Decivilization," *The American Political Science Review*, volume LIII (1959)
Freud, *Civilization and Its Discontents*
Camus, *The Rebel*
Brown, *Life Against Death*
Fingarette, *The Self in Transformation*

(III)

The Meaning of Mental Illness

Is mental illness a scientifically valid concept? One criticism of the term suggest that the medical model of organic disease is inappropriate for ological disorder. What are the practical ications of this model for the involuntary mmitment of those who seem to be mentally ill?

Examine various theories of mental illness in an effort to establish fair criteria for placing people in mental institutions. Use legal as well as sociological studies of the rights of the institutionalized patient.

Szasz, *The Myth of Mental Illness*
Goffman, *Asylums*
Scheff, *Mental Illness and Social Processes*

(II)

The Validity of Social Role Consensus

Early work on the concept of the social role assumes a general consensus on the requirements of specific and generalized social roles, but contemporary studies reflect a diffusion of expectation and an inability to make it concrete. How valid is the assumption of defined social roles today? To what extent have role definitions changed because of subtle shifts in social structure that that allowed change in role definers?

Compare several specific roles that are stereotyped by the mass media. Determine how specific a useful and realistic model for a role can be. Using parallel evidence from an earlier generation, document significant changes in role expectations.

Komarovsky, *Women in the Modern World*
Coleman, *The Adolescent Society*
Gross, Mason, and MacEachern, *Explorations in Role Analysis: Studies of the School Superintendent's Role*

(II)

Motivation and Behavior

Human motivations and reactions relate both the development of the individual psyche and the interaction of the individual with the expectations and role values of the larger society. What are the major personal and social sources of motivation in American society?

Explore sociological theories of motivation. Pay special attention to the achievement motive; affiliation, love, and sex motives; the power-aggression motive; and relevant biological and cognitive theories.

Bindra and Stewart, *Motivation*
McClelland, *The Achieving Society*
Teevan and Birney, *Theories of Motivation in Personality and Social Psychology*

(III)

Group Psychology in Business Organization

Studies in the psychological dimensions of task-oriented groups are of specific relevance for the problem-solving functions of small groups in business. How are such studies relevant to the businessman's need to solve certain types of problems by reaching group conclusions?

Compare recent studies of task-oriented and non-task-oriented groups. Examine particularly group leadership, group mythologies and symbols, and competitive versus cooperative interactive styles.

Freud, *Group Psychology and the Analysis of the Ego*
Slater, *Microcosm*
Bales, *Personality and Interpersonal Behavior*

(II)

.adman and the Genius

.osophers as well as psychologists claim that .ere is an inherently close connection between .nadness and genius, for creative and psychotic thinking seem very similar. Both include peculiar associations, diffuse attention, loose structure, and a variety of regressive modes. What then distinguishes psychotic hallucination from non-pathological creative thinging? Why is this distinction necessary?

Consider the various aspects of phenomenological experience in the mentally ill. Examine both first-hand and clinical accounts.

Kaplan, *The Inner World of Mental Illness*
Laing, *The Divided Self*
Stern, *The Abnormal Person and His World*

(I)

Public Spectacles of Horror

Tortures, executions, fiery sermons about hell and damnation, bloody fights, and gory sports always have provided the most intense entertainment for the masses. Why and how do such painful and dangerous events appeal to spectators? Do such spectacles have a positive socio-psychological function other than entertainment?

In the light of such horrific specacles, reconsider the very concept of entertainment to see whether it must be defined as something more basic and ambivalent than amusement. If so, sketch the main points of the new definition.

Schneider, *The Puritan Mind*
Huizinger, *The Waning of the Middle Ages*
Tertullian, *De Spectacularis*
Fromm, *Escape from Freedom*

(II)

Concepts of Identity

Identity is the crucial issue in contemporary theories of personality, much as sexuality was the crucial issue in Freud's time. How does sexuality relate to current concepts of identity? What are the implications of the shift in emphasis from one to the other?

Examine major theories of identity to discover differences and similarities. Show exactly what each theory means by "identity." Describe the different sources for identity proposed by each theory and discuss the relationship of identity to individual interaction with society.

Erikson, *Identity, Youth, and Crisis*
Allport, *Personality*
Sullivan, *The Interpersonal Theory of Psychiatry*

(II)

Mass Ecstasy and Politics

Much of Nazi power was rooted in the mass experience of the rally. Yet the texts of the speeches delivered at these rallies are insignificant in comparison to the scale, trappings, ritual, and rhythm of the spectacle. What then were the mechanics of the technique that produced in millions of people a commitment that rational appeals never would have produced?

In analyzing writings and movies dealing with these events, take note of how the non-rational elements of the presentation affected the spectators. Draw as many parallels as possible between these rallies and primitive rituals, relying on the presence of ecstatic behavior in both.

Shirer, *The Rise and Fall of the Third Reich*
Bullock, *Hitler—A Study in Tyranny*
Riefenstahl, *Triumph of the Will* (film) and, to a lesser degree, *Olympia*

(I)

The Stages of Human Development

Erikson and Sullivan analyze the life cycle in very different ways, despite superficial similarities in their theories. What are the underlying differences? How do the major themes of traditional psychoanalytic thought differ from those of interpersonal theory, and why?

Examine the fundamental construction of both psychoanalytic orientations, concentrating on concepts of identity, anxiety, socialization, and ego integrity at each stage of development specified by the different theories.

Erikson, *Childhood and Society*
Sullivan, *The Interpersonal Theory of Psychiatry*
Lidz, *The Person: His Development Throughout His Life Cycle*

(III)

The Appeal of Authoritarianism

According to Fromm, authoritarian societies arise when the social climate demands them, when feelings of impotence, inferiority, and aloneness make it necessary to sacrifice personal responsibility for an external authority that can restore meaning and order to society. How well does this theory explain German fascism?

Study social conditions in Germany immediately before Hitler's rise to power in order to test Fromm's theory. Determine whether Nazism was an historical anomaly in Germany or a genuine cultural alternative.

Fromm, *Escape From Freedom*
Schneebaum, *Hitler's Social Revolution: Class and Status in Nazi Germany*
Shirer, *The Rise and Fall of the Third Reich*

(II)

Allport versus Freud?

The basic concepts of Allport's theoretical framework are supposed to have been a direct rebuttal of Freud's psychoanalytic theory. Is this thesis true? How might the theories of Allport and Freud be synthesized for their mutual profit?

Discuss the fundamental concepts of both theories, paying special attention to Allport's treatment of motivation and anxiety. Show how Freud's concepts either parallel or contradict these approaches. Try to evaluate Allport's real contribution to psychoanalytic theory.

Allport, *Becoming: Basic Considerations for a Psychology of Personality*
Freud, *New Introductory Lectures in Psychoanalysis* and *The Ego and the Id*

(III)

Social Psychology of Totalitarian Organizations

What are the common elements of totalitarian organizations? Can you construct a model for such organizations that shows all the relevant social psychological factors? What are the common points of social psychological leverage? How are social activities manipulated, and with what effects?

Consider data on Chinese Communist POW camps, American Foresight salesman training programs, and thought reform centers. Consider the influence of group membership, interpersonal relations, and the individual's need to know, make sense of, and partially control various elements of his environment.

Lifton, *Thought Reform and the Psychology of Totalitarianism*
Goffman, *Asylums*
Freud, *Group Psychology and the Analysis of the Ego*

(II)

Religion and Suicide

What ideological and sociological reasons for suicide supplement and influence more purely personal motives? Does religion relate to suicide and suicidal tendencies in any significant way, either negative or positive?

Study the religious background of people who attempt and commit suicide. Explain how the impact of religion on the individual can be determined, and suggest the implications of the religion-suicide relationship for religion's role in society.

Durkheim, *Suicide*
Morphey, "Religion and Attempted Suicide," *International Journal of Social Psychiatry*, Summer, 1968
Ferracuti, "Suicide in a Catholic Country," and Silving, "Suicide and Law," in *Clues to Suicide* (eds. Faberow and Shneidman)

(I)

Authority and Obedience

Milgram's classic study of conditions of obedience and disobedience suggests fascinating and disturbing aspects of human personality a havior. Most audiences that view films of gram's experiment laugh uncontrollably at vari points, but their laughter is not necessarily relate to laughter occurring in the film. In the context of various analyses of Milgram's experiment, what does this reaction mean?

Use *Psychological Abstracts* to find recent material about the Milgram experiment. Examine other analyses of behavior under stress and note the use of laughter as an indicator of discomfort. Consider the nature of the moral conflict subjects face in this experiment and how laughter relates to that conflict.

Milgram, "Group Pressure and Action Against a Person," *Journal of Abnormal and Social Psychology*, no. 69, 1964, "Some Conditions of Obedience and Disobedience to Authority," in *Current Studies in Social Psychology* (eds. Steiner and Fishbein)
Cohen, *Attitude Change and Social Influence*

(II)

Motivation Correlates and Social Behavior

Clinical psychologists have proposed three major modes of motivation in social interaction: achievement, affiliative, and power-aggression. What areas of human behavior are slighted when the social psychologist considers only these modes? How are these modes related to each other in the motivational process?

Examine a variety of psychological measuring devices, including projective measures of the three motivational modes listed above. Discuss the variety of ways in which achievement is expressed within a given society.

and Veroff, *A Projective Measure of Need for* *iliation*
y and Teevan, *Measuring Human Motivation*
lelland, *The Achieving Society*

(III)

Interpersonal Style and Individual Motivation

Categorizing behavior into various modes of interpersonal style can help to explain individual motivation. What are some possible criteria for an analysis of style? What are the advantages and disadvantages of considering both conscious and unconscious processes?

Compare various formulations of interpersonal style and attempt to analyze the major differences in interpersonal behavior. Support your arguments with data gathered through objective personality tests such as the MMPI and TAT batteries.

Shapiro, *Neurotic Styles*
Lazare, Klerman, and Armor, "Oral, Obsessive, and Hysterical Personality Patterns," *Archives of General Psychology*, volume 14, 1966
Goffman, *Interaction Ritual*

(III)

The Possibility of Sanity

Fromm, Brown, and Freud approach the question of cultural sanity from three quite different standpoints. Which view seems most valid to you, and why?

In comparing the work of these three authors, show first how Fromm evaluates different social systems on the basis of their potentials for cultural sanity, and then how his approach con with Freud's. In comparing Fromm and Bro show how much of their utopian theories is base on truly viable alternatives to the modern situation.

Fromm, *The Sane Society* and *Escape from Freedom*
Freud, *Civilization and Its Discontents*
Brown, *Life Against Death*

(II)

Culture—Past and Present

Society in Comparative and Historical Perspective

Slavery and the Black Man

How did the black man adapt to slave life in the United States? What were the different, specific adaptations? Did they vary according to whether the black man was a field hand, a domestic slave, or another kind of slave? How did these adaptations affect the black man's personality?

Show how Goffman's book relates to this question and to Elkins' thesis. Determine the validity of Elkins' concentration camp analogy and state the historical evidence that might refute it.

Goffman, *Presentation of Self in Everyday Life*
Elkins, *Slavery*
Douglass, *Narrative of the Life of a Slave*

(II)

eval Love

e society of the late Middle Ages seems to have een possessed by "love fever." The noble lady was the focus of an elaborate chivalric ethic that was torn between the values of religion and feudal loyalty, ascetecism and illicit passion. To what extent was this paroxysm of love a product of cultural repression through the Church, and to what extent a result of feudalism's social structure?

Examine the cultural and social conditions of the period as well as typical literature—love poems, chivalric rules, and chronicles or romances.

Hauser, *Social History of Art*—volume I
Huizinga, *The Waning of the Middle Ages*
Ross, ed., *The Portable Medieval Reader*
Collins, *Memoirs of a Medieval Woman*

(II)

The Structure of Organizations in Other Times and Places

Most studies of organizational structure have concentrated on modern, industrial organizations, but a satisfactory characterization of this structure should include studies of all forms of organizations. How do organizations of other times and places compare with contemporary industrial organizations? Do they seriously contradict any generally accepted notions of organizational structure?

Analyze both the Buddhist *sangha* and the monastic orders of the middle ages. Pay attention to particular factors like power structure, bureau-

cracy, stratification, and the possibility c
from within.

Evers, *The Buddhist Sangha in Ceylon and Thailan*
Evans, *Monastic Life at Cluny*
Powicke, *The Christian Life in the Middle Ages*

(II)

Symphony and Factory in the Nineteenth Century

According to Mumford, the mode of organization required to coordinate production in the factory at the time of the Industrial Revolution led to the creation of the symphony. How valid is this thesis?

Compare the scale, type of control, and time-space relationships of the symphony and the factory. Note parallel developments in the other arts and determine whether Industrialism generally influenced modes of perception and expression. Indicate the specific channels through which Industrialism came to affect men's minds.

Mumford, *Technics and Civilization*
Cooke, *Introduction to the History of Factory Systems*
Einstein, *Music in the Romantic Era*

(II)

Female Liberation

What are the premises of the female liberation movement? Why do some women feel the need to be liberated? From what do they want to be liberated?

Consider this movement in socio-historical perspective. Detail the roles that women play in different societies and the ways in which they are socialized to play these roles. State whether

, roles are necessarily confining and un-
.ıg or only seem that way when women
ι male standards for ego-evaluation.

ngdon, *A Short History of Women*
riedan, *The Feminine Mystique*
Levy, *The Family Revolution in Modern China*
de Beauvoir, *The Second Sex*

(III)

Witchcraft—Social Product or Independent Phenomenon?

What were the social factors in the rise of witchcraft? Can it be explained by social psychology, religion, or social structure alone—or should one consider all of these factors?

Compare witchcraft in fourteenth century Europe with witchcraft in Puritan New England. Analyze both the social conditions and the ideologies of these two cultures. Specify the role of the social structure in each case.

Gluckman, *Closed Systems and Open Minds*
Main, *Witchcraft*
Huxley, *The Devils of Loudon*
Warner, *A Black Civilization*
Williams, *Witchcraft*

(II)

Immigrants in America

The study of immigration is an important part of the study of cultural interaction. When and how did the different waves of immigration to America occur? What were the reasons for these movements? How did "native" Americans respond to them?

Consider the problems that immigrants faced and how their backgrounds enabled them to adapt to the problems. Show how the "native" response changed over the years, and detail the tangible results of these changes as well as their effects on the immigrants. Discuss how the immigrant family adapted to America and the implications of their adaptation for American tolerance.

Handlin, *Boston's Immigrants* and *The Uprooted*
Riis, *How the Other Half Lives*
Hingham, *Strangers in the Land*
Davidson, *Life in America*

(III)

The Confrontation of Indian and European Cultures

European settlers found America inhabited by peoples with a culture of their own, the nature of which was radically and fundamentally different from the settlers'. What were the short- and long term effects of this cultural confrontation? Why was there so little productive interaction in the long run?

Detail the extent, depth, and kind of interaction between these opposed cultures. Indicate cultural factors that were decisive in the history of this confrontation.

Josephy, *The Indian Heritage of America* and *Patriot Chiefs*
Soustelle, *Daily Life of the Aztecs*
Washburn, ed., *Indian and White Man*

(II)

The Rise of Bureaucracy

The turn to a bureaucratic, presumably efficient organization of American life had its roots in the

Progressive era. What was the philosophy behind this drive? What institutional arangements did bureaucracy replace? How did the change affect both the individual and the quality of American society?

Discuss the major themes of both Croly's and Lippmann's work. Show what needs these authors felt to be filled by bureaucracy and indicate specific ways in which bureaucracy transformed American life.

Croly, *The Promise of American Life*
Lippmann, *Drift and Mastery*
Wiebe, *Search for Order*

(I)

The Spectator and Social Impotence

How valid is the thesis that in times of social disintegration, vicarious entertainment like spectator sports seems to prevail over participatory entertainment like harvest homes and carnivals?

Compare the Roman and the contemporary fascination with the "hippodrome"—violent spectacles like gladiatorial contests and football games. Decide whether such secondhand involvement, such emotional dependence on someone else's actions, is typical of a certain kind of society in which the common man is alienated from the realm of morally, politically, or physically significant action.

Hamilton, *The Roman Way*
Mumford, *Technics and Civilization*
Davidson, *Life in America*

(II)

Mohammed and Arabian Women

Mohammed was considered a great protector of women, for he urged the improvement of their welfare, protection, and status. Yet he still permitted polygamy and reclusive behavior. Why was this so?

Show how Arabia's social structure in Mohammed's time provoked his concern for women and yet dictated the kind of limited reforms that he could support realistically. Indicate how Mohammed reconciled his ideas with social conditions and managed to manipulate social constants to his advantage.

Levy, *An Introduction to the Sociology of Islam*
Roberts, *The Social Laws of the Qoran*
Lammens, *Islam, Beliefs and Institutions*
Gibb, *Mohammedanism*

(II)

Peaceful and Revolutionary Change

What are the conditions which assure that a redistribution of power within a given society will be accomplished through peaceful rather than revolutionary action?

Compare the alignment of social forces in the French Revolution with their alignment in the English Reform Bill of 1832. Try to demonstrate the general laws and constants of change in each case.

Moore, *The Social Origins of Dictatorship and Democracy*
See "French Revolution" and "English Reform Bill" in the *International Encyclopedia of the Social Sciences*

(II)

The Price of Revolution

Can you develop criteria to evaluate the price of revolution? Or must you simply compare the results to the objectives that were stated initially? Is the position that "cost is no object" in a revolution a viable one?

In treating these questions, pay attention to other operative values like human life, standards of living, types of freedom, etc. Decide whether the benefits of a revolution can be calculated precisely enough to warrant major upheavals, bloodshed, and the destruction of institutions that, no matter how repressive, still functioned for the common good.

Myrdal, *Report From a Chinese Village*
Hinton, *Fanshen*
Moore, *Terror and Progress in the Soviet Union*
Grossman, *The God That Failed*

(III)

Stratification of Village Societies in India

Much of the literature on stratification deals with urban, industrial societies, and thus is both biased and incomplete. In analyzing a qualitatively different social system, do you find that the basic premises of the literature remain valid? Or do they depend too much on their context?

Analyze the study of five Indian villages cited below. State specifically whether elements of stratification in those societies differ radically from the major elements in ours. Bring out the relative importance of these elements to the social structure of the village, and suggest any necessary revisions in current views of stratification.

Haswell, *Economics of Development in Village India*
Mandelbaum, "Status Seeking in Indian Villages," *Transaction*, April, 1968

(II)

The Social Status of the Artist in History

Religion, social organization, and economics all have influenced the status of the plastic artist. What have been the major reasons for rejection or acceptance of the artist, and how have they influenced societal behavior toward the artist?

Concentrate on fifteenth century Italy. Show how the artist's status increased because of his services to fame-seeking banker-princes. Show how the visual arts were glorified because of cultural preoccupation with the value of beauty, the temporal nature of life, and the examples of antiquity.

Burckhardt, *The Civilization of the Renaissance in Italy*
Hauser, *Social History of Art*
Vasari, *The Lives of Painters, Sculptors, and Architects*

(I)

Islamic and Roman Law

The characteristic principle of Islamic law is its divine origin, which is supposed by Moslems to give it greater authority, stability, and perfection than any other law. How does Islamic law compare, functionally and conceptually, with Roman law? Can secular edicts be as effective as religious ones? What are the differences in execution of these laws?

Concentrate on the origins, social impact, and efficacy of Roman and Islamic law. Show how the difference in their reputed sources affects their social power and the flexibility with which they are interpreted.

Gibb, *Mohammedanism*
Wolff, *Roman Law*
Wormser, *The Story of the Law* (revised edition)

(II)

Caste and Race in the American South

The Southern racial "system" is so monolithic and restrictive that some observers have been tempted to call it a caste system. How useful is this designation in your attempts to understand the Southern racial "system"?

Compare this system with a classical caste system like India's. Show how Dollard's study is outdated and how recent developments have changed the system. Sketch the part that "Jim Crow" laws played in the formation of the Southern system.

Dollard, *Caste and Class in a Southern Town*
Woodward, *The Strange Career of Jim Crow*
Basham, *The Wonder that Was India*

(II)

The Rise of Law in Medieval Europe

With the rise of the urban class, trial by fire and water was replaced by written laws that were more relevant means of deciding penal and business matters. How much did this reform owe to changes in social structure? Can you discover specific correlations between legal reform and social development?

Detail the social and economic impact of the rise of the bourgeoisie. Show how much the reinvention of law owed to social pressures and how much to intellectual advances.

Thomson, *Economic and Social History of the Middle Ages*
Pirenne, *Economic and Social History of Medieval Europe*
Ullman, *Principles of Government and Politics*

(II)

Eunuchs in Byzantium

Eunuchs—usually thought to be the deprived parasites of a royal household—were vital functionaries in the Byzantine empire, and parents often castrated their children to ensure them of high position. What explanations can you offer for this anomaly?

Describe the status of eunuchs in Byzantine society and show how their position was a product of factors peculiar to that culture. Explore the dynastic social and political structures of this culture and indicate how one influenced the other. Draw parallels when possible.

Runciman, *Byzantine Civilization*
Psellus, *Fourteen Byzantine Rulers*
Procopius, *Secret History*
Hussey, *The Byzantine World*

(II)

Women in Antiquity

How well do women's rights, treatment, and place in a society reflect that society's real *conception of freedom and its definition of man, in contrast to overtly supported (male) values?*

Examine the position of women in Classical Greece. Show how it conformed or conflicted with the prevailing humanistic ideals of this period.

Muller, *Freedom in the Ancient World*
Dewey, *Freedom and Culture*
Langdon, *A Short History of Women*
Seltman, *Women in Antiquity*

(II)

Demonstrations Today and Yesterday

Are demonstrations just a disease of modern society? What do today's riots and demonstrations have in common with those of earlier centuries? What are the differences, and how can you account for them?

Compare demonstrations on medieval campuses with those on U.S. campuses in the 1960's. Concentrate on issues, methods, involvement of outsiders, results, and punishments.

Daedalus, Winter, 1968—*The Embattled University*
Cohen and Hale, eds., *The Berkeley Student Revolt*
Schachner, *The Medieval Universities*
Harknis, *The Rise of the Universities*

(I)

The Social Impact of Mining

How did mining affect, not the economics, but the structure and institutions of the society that relied on it?

Show how the routine, environment, and living standards of mining were transferred to the larger society after they developed in the mining village. Indicate how mining may have affected the growth of factories, urban slums, and popular pleasures.

Mumford, *Technics and Civilization*
Stanley, *The Coal Question* and *Men, Machines, and History*

(II)

Carnivals

Some societies celebrate carnival (carne vale—*farewell to flesh, the coming of Lent) at greater length and with greater intensity than others. How does the form and importance of such celebration depend on the structure and the degree of industrialization of a society?*

Compare carnival in the northern United States with Latin American and contemporary Greek celebrations. Suggest whether the differences stem from variations in job structure, scale of society, and outlets for sex and ego needs.

Eliade, *The Sacred and the Profane*
Megas, *Greek Calendar Customs*
Crow, *Spanish American Life*
Ewbank, *Life in Brazil*

(II)

The Artist and His Public

The effortless enjoyment of art has become rare as the distance between the artist and his audience has increased. What accounts for this development? How much is it the result of the artist's reflecting accelerated technological and cultural change?

Try to synthesize the theories of the authors cited below. To establish the relationship of the contemporary artist and his public, document the content and approach of art magazines, the way newspapers usually present art news, and both the prices and locations of art works today.

Rosenberg, *The Tradition of the New*
Read, *The Redemption of the Robot*
Hauser, *Social History of Art*, volumes II and IV
Boorstin, *The Image*

(III)

Nat Turner: Man and Myth

An important controversy arose over the publication of The Confessions of Nat Turner. *How did this controversy reflect the widening gap between black and white, and what were the operant factors in this divergence?*

Compare the attitudes of Bontemps and Styron toward their material. Demonstrate the differences of their approaches. Detail the major objections to Styron's work that were voiced in *Ten Black Writers Respond* and discuss their implications for historical and sociological research.

Bontemps, *Black Thunder*
Styron, *The Confessions of Nat Turner*
Clarke, ed., *Ten Black Writers Respond*

(II)

Guild and Union

Both the guild and the union were formed to protect the artisan or worker financially, medically, and socially, but their organization differed greatly. How did their provisions, rules, assumptions, and power grow from both the economic and the social systems that spawned them? How do their different organizations reflect the differing organization and values of their social contexts?

Bring out differences in the depth and humanity of the care that unions and guilds accorded their members. Determine whether guilds and unions differ only in bureaucracy or in their different assumptions about needs and human freedom. Account for these differences by referring to the social context.

Pirenne, *Medieval Cities, Their Origins, and the Revival of Trade*
Boissonnade, *Life and Work in Medieval Europe*
Burke, *The History and Functions of Central Labor Unions*

(II)

Gifts

Americans attach so much importance to gift rituals that even poor families feel obliged to buy presents far beyond their means and to give gifts frequently. Is this an indication of America's increasingly "economic" and decreasingly "sacro-social" attitude toward gifts?

Compare this gift ritual to primitive exchange rituals in order to find the original meaning of gifts. Consider whether the apparently mercenary nature of American gift rituals is a strong attempt at social cohesion.

Levi-Strauss, "The Principle of Reciprocity," in *Sociological Theory* (ed. Cosen)
Malinowski, *Crime and Custom in Savage Society*
Mauss, *The Gift*

(II)

Madness in History

Irrational behavior has influenced history as much as rational or "rationalized" activities. What were the forms and intensity of such behavior during two different periods of history? What ideological and social factors determined madness during each period, and what were the final effects on society?

Consider group behavior that has been characterized as mad at different times and show why what was "insane" at one time was perfectly "rational" at another. Compare Classical Greek and Medieval forms of madness.

Foucault, *Madness and Civilization*
Dodds, *The Greeks and the Irrational*
Huizinga, *The Waning of the Middle Ages*

(I)

Cooperation and Competition

American capitalist society assumes that competition is a "natural" form of behavior, inherent to human nature and the struggle for survival. Is such an assumption universally true, or does it simply reflect provincial predilections?

Compare American society to different cultures that do not base interaction on competition. Determine whether such other bases are more efficient and more conductive to mental health.

Crafts, *Cooperation and Competition*
Mead, *Competition and Cooperation Among Primitive Peoples*

(I)

The Social Functions of Funeral Rites

Many sociologists contend that although funeral rites focus on the dead, they are primarily designed for the living. They are supposed to perform a variety of social, psychological, and cultural functions for the community, such as adjustment to loss and contact with the supernatural. Does this view of funeral rites hold true cross-culturally? If so, what basic principles emerge?

Use Mandelbaum's article as a point of departure. In comparing funeral rites among historical and contemporary societies, concentrate on function, effectiveness, and degree of elaboration.

Mandelbaum, "The Social Uses of Funeral Rites," in *The Meaning of Death* (ed. Feifel)
Volkart, "Bereavement and Mental Health," in *Explorations in Social Psychiatry* (eds. Leighton, Clausen, and Wilson)
Giesey, *The Royal Funeral Ceremony in Renaissance France* (unpublished doctoral dissertation, University of California at Berkeley)
Puckle, *Funeral Customs*
Bendamm, *Death Customs*

(II)

The Origins, Structure, and Process of Modern Society

Alienation and Modern Society

Alienation frequently is used to describe the social condition of modern man. What exactly does the term mean? How has its meaning and use changed during the last hundred years?

Compare and contrast Marx's use of the term with that of the existentialist philosophers. Determine how and how much alienation corresponds with industrialization. State whether alienation really is useful as a sociological concept, and show how Kenniston sees the problem as one that relates to the position of youth in modern society.

Kenniston, *The Uncommitted*
Josephson, *Man Alone*
Kaufmann, *Existentialism from Dostoevsky to Sartre*
Marx, *Economic and Philosophic Manuscripts*

(II)

The Hippie—Against or Out of Society?

What is the position of the hippie sub-culture in the social system? Is it a class, or does it represent the destruction of class distinctions? Is such a destruction possible in contemporary society? Or does the scale and complexity of modern industrial society prevent both total escape (as in communes) and the destruction of class lines?

Consider these questions in light of criticisms of hippies and of hippie ideology itself. Determine how much hippies are a part and product of society and how viable their proposed solutions are.

Yablonsky, *The Hippie Trip*
Hopkins, *The Hippie Papers*
Berger, *A Rumor of Angels*
Also, periodical literature and movies (*Easy Rider*)

(I)

Contemporary Rites

What rites are most elaborate in contemporary American society? Does the primitive stress on rites of birth, initiation, marriage, and death still prevail? Do the cultural repression of death and the secularization of marriage mean that those rites have become less important?

Examine the rites that accompany the above occasions to determine whether they are real or empty. Decide whether other events of the life cycle now evoke more attention and involve more significant rites or whether the overwhelming variety of modern experience has reduced the intensity of all archetypical occasions.

Eliade, *Myth and Reality* and *The Sacred and the Profane*
Van Genner, *Rites of Passage*

Thomson, *Hell's Angels*
McLuhan, *War and Peace in the Global Village*

(II)

The Community and the Police

How does the official function of the police contrast with its actual function? Are there major discrepancies? If so, what are they, and how have they developed?

Consider how the police function in a radical or liberal community within the framework of a conservative society and show how they change from being a protective force to being a repressive and aggressive agent of the larger framework.

Gardner, *Cops on Campus and Crimes in the Streets*
Hayden, *Rebellion and Repression*
Connery, *Urban Riots*
Report of the National Commission on Civil Disorders

(II)

The Women's Liberation Movement

Why did this movement develop when it did? How is it related to other movements that seek basic solutions to problems of oppression and prejudice? How does the Women's Liberation Movement differ in its premises and tactics from other, similar movements in history?

Place this movement in its historical context and show in what ways—theory, polemics, targets, and solutions—it is unique and in what ways a repetition of previous movements. Suggest how psycho-social conditions in contemporary America have contributed to the actual origin of this movement.

Flexner, *A Century of Struggle*
de Beauvoir, *The Second Sex*
Whyte, *Street Corner Society*
Romm, *The Open Conspiracy*
Bird, *Born Female*

(I)

The Pornography of Death

In contemporary American society, natural death is a taboo, and direct references to it are thought shocking and obscene. Thus any confrontation with death has a pornographic quality.

Using Gorer's article as a point of departure, examine families, newspapers, funeral homes, etc. for their attitudes toward, references to, and treatment of death. Then compare the ritual and consequences of death in America with those in another country. Decide whether Gorer's thesis is valid.

Gorer, "The Pornography of Death," *Modern Writing*, 1955, pps. 56-62; and *Death, Grief, and Mourning*

(II)

The Existence of Subcultures

The theory of subcultures is among the most widely used and most harshly criticized concepts of modern sociology. Most often used to explain the development of juvenile delinquency, it has implications for other forms of social deviance as well. In a discussion of juvenile delinquency, how would you reconcile Cohen's theory of subcultures with Miller's theory of lower class culture? What are the broader implications of your synthesis?

In examining and reconciling these theories, pay special attention to Matza's critique and others.

To verify these theories, use recent studies on the cultural reinforcing agents of juvenile delinquency.

Matza, *Delinquency and Drift*
Cohen, *Deviance and Control*
Miller, "Lower Class Culture as a Generating Milieu of Gang Delinquency," *Journal of Social Issues*, 1958.

(III)

Poverty and the Ghetto

From the beginning of its urbanization, affluent America has included islands of poverty, backwardness, and misery. Attempts to reform these islands have shown that the ghetto is a peculiarly resistant one. Why? What methods are most appropriate to relieving poverty in the ghetto?

Discuss ghetto culture and its emotional, economic, and social relationships with the culture that surrounds it. Show how these relationships affect ghetto poverty and attempts to relieve it.

Hapgood, *The Spirit of the Ghetto*
Harrington, *The Other America*
Sinion, *Faces of Poverty*
Clark and Hopkins, *A Relevant War on Poverty*

(III)

The Communications Revolution

Some theorists feel that the communications revolution can resolve contemporary political and social conflict. Others feel that this effect is negligible when compared with the revolution's destructive effects on creative thought. How valid are these opposed arguments?

Suggest controls that might reinforce communications of all technological types in ways that would benefit both the individual and his political community.

Copes, *Communication or Conflict*
McLuhan, *The Medium is the Massage*
Marcuse, *One Dimensional Man*

(II)

Folkways Today

According to Sumner, folkways are modes of action (usually petty, everyday action) that make up most of the activities we perform, leaving little margin for rational, voluntary action. They are the products of the mass sub-conscious in its search for answers to the primary needs of hunger, sex, vanity, and fear.

Choose a fraction of a typical day's time on television and analyze the actors' dress, speech, manners, and activities. Point out which of these are the product of folkways and their resulting mores and which seem to be unpredictable, individual, "free" behavior.

Sumner, *Folkways*
McLuhan, *The Mechanical Bride*

(I)

American Cities

What are the economic, political, and cultural functions of cities in the United States?

Examine a broad range of material dealing with the functions of the city, and then develop your own, independent stance. Discuss how interdependent and/or contradictory these functions are and whether they seem to have permanent effects on the structure of society.

Jacobs, *The Economy of Cities*
Alexanderson, *The Industrial Structure of American Cities*
Riess, "Functional Specialization of Cities," in *Cities and Society*
Alexander, *An Economic Base Study of Madison*

(II)

Toward a New Concept of Society

Buckminster Fuller's "World Game," the preoccupation with ecology, the emergence of peace and anti-nationalist movements, and the increasing anti-militarism of most sophisticated societies seem to support McLuhan's contention that the world is becoming a global village closely connecting the interests of all people and demanding new ways of dealing with society.

Closely study the works of McLuhan, Fuller, and McHarg to determine whether they are surrealistic prophecies or rational analyses rooted in real social conditions. Critically examine the validity and feasibility of their proposals in sociological terms.

McLuhan, *Understanding Media*
Fuller, *No More Secondhand Gods* and *Utopia or Oblivion*
McHarg, *Multiply and Subdue the Earth*

(II)

Poverty and Affluence in America

America often is characterized as the "affluent society." How true is this characterization? What evidence is there to the contrary?

Show how Harrington's book was a breakthroug

and why it appeared when it did and not five years earlier. State how and why poverty is itself a culture.

Harrington, *The Other America*
Caudill, *Night Comes to the Cumberlands*
Gladwin, *Poverty USA*

(I)

The Industrial State and Ideology

As a political system develops into a highly industrialized modern state, does its ideological commitment become less relevant? Do people, particularly political leaders, start to neglect or ignore the values on which the system was based in its early years?

Study this problem in both capitalist and socialist systems. Try to bring out specific forces—social legislation, aggregate economies, etc.—that might affect ideological commitment in the large industrial state.

Bell, *The End of Ideology*
Moore, *Terror and Progress*

(III)

Contemporary Elites

What are the social functions of self-consciously styled contemporary artistic-cultural-philosophic elites? Do they simply express distaste for mass society and insulate themselves from society, or do they provide examples of alternative life-styles that will change society in the long run?

Examine such elites in their historical and mythological context. Concentrate on one of them, like the avant-garde artists. In reviewing their literature, work, and social behavior, try to see how much they may already have affected society. Use Simmel as a springboard for discussion.

Simmel, "The Sociology of Secret Societies," in *The Sociology of Georg Simmel* (ed. Watt)
Camus, *The Rebel*
Eliade, *Myth and Reality*

(II)

Technology and Contemporary Man

What is the nature of technology, both as a technique and as a state of mind? What do contemporary authors fear about technology? And what problems does it really represent to modern man?

Critically examine Ellul's characterization of technology and its dangers. Discuss the validity of Roszak's identification of technology with "science" in general, and state how effectively Bronowski copes with criticisms of the scientific outlook.

Ellul, *Technological Society*
Roszak, *The Making of a Counter Culture*
Bronowski, *Science and Human Values*

(II)

Black in America

One way to survey the rise of self-consciousness among black Americans is to study their literature. How has the focus of black literature changed since the 1930's?

Compare and contrast *Native Son* and *Another Country* to show how they reflect the periods in which they were written. State what Ellison means by "invisible man" and how Baldwin views the concept of "native son." Conclude by demonstrating how this selection of black literature reflects the black experience over the last several decades.

Wright, *Native Son*
Ellison, *Invisible Man*
Baldwin, *Notes of a Native Son* and *Another Country*
Kearns, *The Black Experience*

(I)

Prophets

Many non-religious thinkers today seem to share the ancient prophet's prestige and appeal to large groups of society, as well as the hatred and antagonism from other groups. Can a real comparison be made between traditional and modern prophets?

Compare McLuhan, Maharishi, and Marcuse with traditional prophets. Decide what binds them together—their concern with culture as a whole, their eschatological outlook, or the way in which they are readily misinterpreted and/or used by the millions. State whether their gospels are more or less theoretical, factual, psychological, or, especially, moral.

McLuhan, *Understanding Media* and *The Medium Is the Massage*
Maharishi Mahesh Yogi, *The Science of Being and the Joy of Living*
Marcuse, *Eros and Civilization*
Weber, *The Sociology of Religion*
Simmel, "The Metropolis and Mental Life," in *The Sociology of Georg Simmel* (ed. Wolff)

(III)

Youth and Contemporary Culture

The phrase "youth culture" has been used frequently since 1960. What does it mean? What does its use reflect about society at large?

Contrast the rebels of the 50's and the 60's and decide how well Kenniston and Roszack understand these phenomena. Show how Ginsberg can be said to bridge the gap between the two decades and discuss the tangible forms the rebellions have taken.

Kenniston, *Young Radicals* and *The Uncommitted*
Roszack, *The Making of a Counter Culture*
Ginsberg, *Howl*

(II)

Black Self Concepts

Self concepts of black separatists differ significantly from those of black integrationists. How are these differences developed and maintained?

Consider studies of the black movements and their ideologies and try to discern specific social, economic, and political factors that account for these differences.

Whyte, *Street Corner Society*
Cleaver, *Soul on Ice*
Malcolm X, *Autobiography of Malcolm X*

(I)

Embourgeoisement: Myth or Reality?

A critical study of a working-class suburb in England suggests that the thesis of middle-class absorption of the working class in technological societies may be false. How valid is the thesis? Why and where does it break down in reality?

Compare Goldethorpe's definition of the working class with Marx's, and show how it affects perception of embourgeoisement. Then, from your own experience, suggest whether this phenomenon is common in America.

Goldethorpe and Lockwood, *The Affluent Worker in the Class Structure*
Avineri, *The Sociology of Marx*

(II)

Early American Cities and Social Change

The appearance of the city in America meant not only an improvement in the standard of living and a difference in physical surroundings, but also a change in the quality of society. How did the advent of cities affect previously existing social structures and attitudes?

In studying the early stages of cities, show how each technological change influenced the inhabitants—how adequate street lighting created night life, how the organization of police forces and firemen affected the neighborhood ethic, etc. Then suggest how and how much urban technology changes social structure.

Davidson, *Life in America*
Mumford, *The City in History* and *The Culture of Cities*

(I)

Bohemia

How successful were American "Bohemians" in their attempts to be free from the establishment? What kind of behavior characterized these attempts, and what forces motivated them?

Study the development of Greenwich Village, originally a Bohemian community. Show how independent it was of the greater urban context. Bring out the inherent difficulties and advantages of such a community.

Stein, *Eclipse of Community*
Ware, *Greenwich Village*
Cowley, *The Exile's Return*

(II)

Cultural Anxiety and Political Decisions

Political decisions influenced by anxiety often are destructive and self-defeating. They also can widen the gap between action and ideology. What are the causes of such decisions? How do the decisions themselves influence those who make them?

Use Neumann's article as a starting point. Decide whether the causes for such decisions can be affected by therapy, better education of the decision-maker, or other means. Decide whether a radical change of the social system is needed instead.

Neumann, *The Democratic and the Authoritarian State*
Fromm, *Escape from Freedom*
Freud, *Group Psychology and the Analysis of the Ego*

(II)

Bureaucratic and Manual Labor

One aim of management is to ensure some degree and kind of "happiness" for the worker. What are the components of this happiness in the eyes of the bureaucratic, in the worker's eyes, and in reality?

Pay particular attention to the worker's moral outlook and show how it affects his "happiness" in his own estimation and in behavioral terms. Show how the worker reacts to different conditions of power structure, quality, organization, ritual, and relevance.

Argyris, *Personality and Organization*
Blauner, *Alienation and Freedom*
Beusman and Rosenberg, "The Meaning of Work in a Bureaucratic Society," in *Identity and Anxiety* (ed. Stein)
Swados, "The Myth of the Happy Worker," *Nation*, CLXXXV, no. 4, 1957

(III)

Natural and Violent Death in America

While Americans seem to repress the phenomenon of natural death, violent death is over-emphasized. News media, the arts, and popular legends often emphasize violent death. Why is this so, and how does the public maintain the dichotomy between these two kinds of death?

Contrast the ways in which the two kinds of death are presented to the public. Try to explore the cultural reasons for the distinction between them.

Gorer, "The Pornography of Death," in *Modern Writing*, 1959, pp. 56-62
Mumford, *The Culture of Cities*

(II)

Two Views of the Lonely Crowd

David Riesman's first book was persuasive and enormously influential in the study of alienation and mass phenomena; yet a decade later, the author changed his mind entirely. Exactly what were these changes? Which of Riesman's views seems most reasonable to you?

Closely study the differences in approach, premises, and results between the two books. State whether these books lead to any prognoses; if so, elaborate.

Riesman *The Lonely Crowd* and *Faces in the Crowd*

(I)

Education for Tomorrow

Herbert Read suggests that the premises of our educational system are outdated, for the system does not prepare people for a society that offers leisure, less repression, and great margin for creative life-styles. He holds that in order to realize such a society, we must discover new educational principles. How valid is Read's argument? And how useful are his suggestions?

Determine whether the new educational premises and methods that Read suggests actually will provide the tool for social, aesthetic, and intellectual reform. Critically evaluate Read's basic assumptions.

Read, *The Redemption of the Robot*
Buber, *Between Man and Man*
Jung, "Two Essays on Analytical Psychology," *Collected Works*, volume 7

(III)

Auto Shows and Renewal

In many ways, annual auto shows are comparable to annual renewal festivals. Their flashiness, the expectation that surrounds them, and their highly ritualistic character all seem to support this comparison. In what ways is the identification of auto shows and renewal rites a valid one?

Compare the symbolic function of these shows with that of ancient festivals, like the Panathenean. Examine the occasion's publicity, appeal, impact on society, and physical and symbolic elements.

Eliade, *Myth and Reality* and *The Sacred and the Profane*
Boorstin, *The Image*
Frazer, *The Golden Bough*
Harrison, *Epilegomena to the Study of Greek Religion* and *Themis*

(I)

Community—A Relevant Concept?

How has the definition of community changed at different times and in different places? Does it still have meaning in our own society, or must we redefine it?

Review changes in the concept of community since Rousseau's time and consider the best and most realistic redefinition for today. Decide whether changes in this definition reveal the impossibility of any community or the necessity of radical interpretaton.

Berlin, *Four Essays on Liberty*
Laing, *The Divided Self*
Wylie, *Village in the Vaucluse*

(II)

Advertisement and the Consumer

Changes in the goods offered and the symbols used in advertisement indicate cultural and eco-

nomic shifts, as well as changes in everyday habits, idealizations, and desires. Does advertisement itself promote such changes, or does it simply adapt to new structural realities?

Analyze the content of advertisements in a broad range of periodicals over a specific period of time. After a general view, concentrate on one area—food, automobiles, etc. Include articles on consumer goods in your analysis.

Hoggart, *The Uses of Literacy*
Journalism Quarterly, *Journal of Advertising Research*, and others

(II)

Mental Life and The Metropolis

The metropolis affects man in more ways than the physical and economic, and even these factors eventually change the urbanite's overall attitudes. Exactly how does the metropolis change man's mind?

Explore the impact of the physical and organizational aspects of the metropolis—lighting, rhythm, lack of open spaces, routine, bureaucracy, scale, construction, consumption, and informational glut—on human conceptions of life, nature, values, and history. Try to establish specific correspondences between certain metropolitan features and certain mental changes.

The Exploding Metropolis (ed. by *Fortune*)
Davidson, *Life in America*
Abrams, *Man's Struggle for Shelter in an Urbanizing World*
Jacobs, *The Death and Life of Great American Cities*

(III)

Camus, The Stranger

Is The Stranger *still a stranger? Or has anomie increased to the point at which behavior originally called deviant is now becoming normal?*

Compare reviews of *The Stranger* when it first appeared with the reactions of its readers today. Try to show how changes in reactions reflect changes in the level of anomie. Interviews with those who recently have read the book are essential.

Camus, *The Stranger*
McMullen, *Art, Affluence and Alienation*

(I)

The Detective Novel and Exemplary Action

Detective novels and movies provide endless entertainment for many harmless, quiet people. What is the nature of this entertainment? What is the nature of the audience's emotional investment in the detective hero compared with its investment in the romantic or the comic hero?

Show the correspondence between detective heroes and mythical (fighter) heroes. Bring out similarities and differences in plot, scale, fantasy, and symbol. Decide whether these heroes perform comparable functions for their audiences.

Eliade, *Myth and Reality*
Campbell, *The Masks of God—Creative Mythology* and *The Hero with a Thousand Faces*
Hamilton, *Mythology*

(I)

The Social Patterns of Suburbia

Despite suburbia's physical distance from the city, suburban attitudes remain close to the heart of the city—suburbia's uniformity of education and class often make it more an abstraction than a diversified, dynamic community. Is this statement valid? If so, in what ways?

Study a small suburban community at first hand, using interviews and questionnaires whenever necessary, but concentrating on observation. Determine whether the suburban orientation is exclusively corporational and whether most formal social groups (clubs, teams, etc.) rest on considerations of status.

Stein, *Eclipse of Community*
Albee, *Everything in the Garden*

(III)

Politics and Alienation

Feelings of alienation and commitment differ significantly among political and non-political students. Is alienation related to the type *of political involvement more than to political involvement* per se?

Observe and interview political and non-political students on your campus to determine which group feels more instrumental to society and how these feelings are expressed in action. Try to correlate political action of different kinds and levels with different feelings and levels of alienation or commitment.

Kunen, *The Strawberry Statement*
Kenniston, *The Uncommitted*

(II)

Theories of Student Unrest

Much attention has centered on student rebellion both here and abroad; and sociologists quickly have developed theories to explain this unrest. Which of these explanations seems most persuasive, and why?

Critically compare the major theories to find out which explain the most aspects of the phenomenon. Decide whether they share any premises that demand reconsideration, and compare them with student writings to discover elements that the theories neglect.

Feur, *The Conflict of Generations*
Kenniston, *The Young Radicals*
Shah, "Student Unrest, a Sociological Hypothesis," *Sociological Bulletin*, March, 1968
Trimberger, "Why a Rebellion at Columbia Was Inevitable," *Transaction*, September, 1968
Cohn-Bendit, *Obsolete Communism*
Bourges, *The French Student Revolt: The Leaders Speak*

(III)

Old Age Homes

American and European attitudes toward old age homes differ greatly. What is a last resort in Europe is common practice here, and economic motives seem to have no influence on such decisions. Exactly what forces pressure the aged and their families to decide in favor of an old age home?

Research: interview and observe the directors of old age homes and their boarders in your area. Try to determine the conditions under which most of the aged arrived at the home. Distinguish between financial and social pressures and find out how much the aged were obliged to enter a home and how much they felt pressured to do so by their families and the rest of society.

(II)

Mobility and Alternating Identies

A more radical shift in self concept occurs among students who go away to college than among commuter students. Is this shift permament? What groups on and off campus facilitate or impede it?

To answer these questions, perform an empirical study based on questionnaires. Make specific reference to the ways in which campus groups and figures substitute for family and community ones.

Berger, *Invitation to Sociology*
Sanford, *The American College*

(I)

Preachers and Pop Singers

During the Middle Ages, preachers were culture heroes whose performances produced both catharsis and religious sentiment. Cases of mass hysteria and hero worship were common. How much does the general impact of these men resemble that of contemporary pop singers? Do they answer similar cultural, social, and psychological needs?

Explore the preacher's and the pop singer's reliance on charisma, flamboyant performance, and mob worship. Try to reach some general conclusions about the public's need for an idol and agent of intoxication.

Weber, *The Sociology of Religion*
Huizinga, *The Waning of the Middle Ages*
Ross, ed., *The Viking Portable Medieval Reader*

(II)

The City and the Country

Until recently, most people held that cities were built on a rural economic base, and that this fact constrained and shaped them in particular ways. But in attempting to improve city planning, many writers have challenged this contention. What are the challenges, and how convincing are they?

Explore Jane Jacob's thesis and the proofs she adduces. Explain exactly why Sennet calls her an urban anarchist and indicate the implications of her thesis for city planning.

Jacobs, *The Death and Life of Great American Cities* and *The Economy of Cities*
Sennet, "Urban Anarchist," *The New York Review of Books*, XIII, January 1, 1970
Handlin, *The Historian and the City*

(II)

Social Mobility in Industrial Society

As industrial society moves into the post-industrial stage, social benefits are spread, the worker buys televisions and cars, and the middle class gradually grows to include him. What are the bases for such a statement? Are they persuasive?

Critically examine Dahrendorf's and Lipset's texts. Assess their evidence, their reasoning, and their conclusions.

Dahrendorf, *Class and Class Conflict in Industrial Society*
Lipset, "The Changing Class Structure and Contemporary European Politics," in *A New Europe* (ed. Graubard)

(III)

Underground Press

The underground press has surfaced so much in our time that it now may represent the cultural milieu as much as the established press does. How does it reflect the culture that it addresses? To what aspects and sectors of society does it give a voice?

Analyze the contents, style, visual aspects, and distribution of some basic examples of the underground press—liberal-artistic magazines, avant-garde publications, scandalous newspapers, pornographic periodicals, and radical political pamphlets. What do they have in common? How does their format vary to accommodate a particular audience? Discuss their social/psychological functions and whether they satisfy widely spread needs, or simply provide escape.

Lowenthal, *Literature, Popular Culture, and Society*
Romm, *The Open Conspiracy*

(II)

Popular Initiation Rites

A most remarkable contemporary example of the secret society is the Hell's Angels motorcycle gang. What is the mythical significance of this group and others like it?

Compare the rites, trappings, secrecy, and solidarity of this group with similar aspects of groups responsible for initiation rites in primitive societies. Suggest why other, more conventional secret societies—like the Masons—recently have failed to function as the administrators initiation rites.

Thompson, *Hell's Angels*
Campbell, *The Masks of God—Primitive Mythology*
Van Genner, *The Rites of Passage*

(II)

Youth and the Revolution

Youth and revolution often have been connected historically, but today they are practically synonomous. Is this close association a distinctly modern phenomenon? What factors make it so close?

Answer these questions through a comparative study of the following texts. Explore the unique reason for the revolutionary commitment of young people and indicate the relationship between this commitment and alienation.

Flacks, *The Liberated Generation*
Daedalus, Winter 1968—*Students and Politics*
Cockl, *Student Power*

(II)

The Social Impact of the Popular Arts

Through the impressiveness of their media, their ubiquity, and the size of their audience, the popular arts affect social conditions in profound and varied ways. How do they affect our daily lives? Do they enrich our experience, or do they inhibit first-hand experience by providing models that cannot be reconciled with reality? What long range social effects seem likely?

Choose a limited kind of human interaction like sexual attraction and romantic love. Show how popular art almost dictates the necessary elements of such interaction—i.e., idyllic background, soft music, sudden and flamboyant discovery of the "other," etc. Decide how much the popular arts actually modify, rather than give expression to the essential elements of such interactions.

Geddes, *The Public Arts*
Warshow, *The Immediate Experience*
Boorstin, *The Image*
McLuhan, *The Mechanical Bride*

(II)

The Search for Community

The scale of industrial, metropolitan life has destroyed community, for it is too large to satisfy the individual's need for intimacy, solidarity, and a stable social milieu. Is the nation state the only possible form of community at this time, or are there viable alternatives?

Show how communes, fraternities, radical groups, and cooperative housing resemble the original type of community. Decide whether they are adequate substitutes and contain solutions applicable to society in general.

Stein, *The Eclipse of the Community*
Wolff, ed., *The Sociology of Georg Simmel*
Laing, *The Divided Self*

(I)

The Changing Uses of Leisure Time

Change in leisure time activities may be a response to various events that allow leisure for a particular class; leisure time activities often are status symbols. How does upward mobility affect the type of leisure activity in which families indulge? How is such activity related to the family structure of various classes? Is there a relationship between type and amount of leisure time activity and the source of leisure time?

Study your own family's leisure time activities and those of your friends' families. Then interview people at bowling alleys, race tracks, and other leisure time resorts, and read journals that deal with leisure time—*Holiday, Gourmet,* etc. Show the connection of such activities with one's ideal concept of himself and with the repressed part of one's personality.

Veblen, *The Theory of the Leisure Class*

(III)

The Paris Student Revolt

Its ideologues often explain a revolt better than its observors do. How valid are the ideological accounts of the French student revolt? What motivations do they bring out, and which ones do they repress?

Compare ideological and sociological studies of the revolt in order to assess the value of the insider's and the outsider's views. Examine the revolt's importance to French society and discuss its sociological dimensions. State whether the revolt was as broadly based and received as its ideologues contend.

Salloch, *In Pursuit of Ideology—The French Student Revolt*
Cohn-Bendit, *Obsolete Communism*
Hobsbawm, "Why France's Revolt Failed," *The New York Review of Books,* May 22, 1969

(II)

Theater and Ritual

Theater in contemporary society has come to occupy a position similar to that of religion in primitive society. What societal and individual needs are fulfilled by both theater and ritual religion? Can the role of the actor be compared to that of the participant in a ritual? Does an audience participate in theater as the community does in ritual religion?

Base your discussion on both the theoretical works of theatrical innovators and the traditional anthropological studies of ritual. Study a particular ritual and attempt to apply theatrical theory to it.

Turner, *Forest of Symbols*
Grotowski, *Toward a Poor Theater*
Artaud, *The Theater and Its Double*

(I)

The Sociological Implications of Participation

The New Left in America feels that participation is necessary in order to break down the subject-object nature of political relationships. Others feel that a radical growth in participatory politics would destroy social harmony by making democratic government impossible. Which view seems more reasonable to you? Are the projected social horrors of participation likely to occur?

Define and compare the differences and the social implications of the conflicting critiques of participation that appear in the works cited below.

Cohn-Bendit, *Obsolete Communism*
Milbrath, *Political Participation*

(II)

The Changing World of the Movies

Like other manifestations of culture, the movies indicate moods, values, and issues of general con-

cern to a specific society. Does a comparison of movies from different decades say very much about changes that have occurred in a society during those periods of time? If so, what does it say, and how articulately?

Choose a movie about war from the thirties (like *Wings*), from the forties (like *Casablanca*), and from the fifties (*The Young Lions*). Analyze plot, character, objectivity, attitudes toward war, and presentation of patriotism versus self-preservation to see how each movie reflects specific characteristics of its decade. Use newspapers and editorials of those decades to establish these characteristics.

Warshow, *The Immediate Experience*

(II)

Meta-Sociology

The Sociology of Knowledge

Marx and the Sociology of Knowledge

Marx argued that systems of thought are determined by the economic structure of society, despite the protests of independent thinkers. Was Marx right? What are the implications of his theory for the sociology of knowledge?

Show exactly how Marx concentrated on economic factors and whether this concentration was justified. State what Marx meant by a "sub-structure" and what his theory implied for the rest of his thought. Indicate how other sociologists have reacted to this thesis.

Marx, *German Ideology*
Engels, *Anti-Duhring*
Curtis and Petras, *Introduction to the Sociology of Knowledge*
Mannheim, *Ideology and Utopia*

(II)

The Moral Capacities of the Lower Class

Homer, Tacitus, and Thucydides consistently attribute base, materialistic motives to lower-class behavior, especially rebellious behavior. But the modern, industrial attitude, seen, for example, in the novels of Dickens, is strikingly different. What are the differences, and why did they develop? What are the social implications of these differences?

Describe and try to explain the differences in terms of various social organizations in pre-industrial societies. Indicate how much weight should be given to the development of Christian thought in the intervening period.

Auerbach, *Mimesis*
Smith, *The Wealth of Nations*
Dickens, *Bleak House* and other novels
Muller, *Freedom in the Ancient World*

(I)

Changing Patterns of Religion

Forms of religion and forms of social structure are interdependent. How do present social structures affect the rise of non-institutionalized religions? How do the messages and social/psycho-

logical appeals of new religions compare with those of older, established religions? Do the differences have real implications for contemporary social structure?

Consider meditation movements, love and peace cults, millenarian movements, and occultism. Determine whether the premises and practices of these two kinds of religion have something in common and to what extent the differences stem from the different kinds of societies that created them. Suggest the constants of human social experience to which the common factors correspond and the radical social changes that the differences reflect.

Yinger, *Sociology Looks at Religion*
Wilson, *Religion in Secular Society*
Lenski, *The Religious Factor*
Berger, *A Rumor of Angels*

(III)

Changing Views of War in Ancient Greece

Homer's view of war differs significantly from the later views of Aeschylus and Euripides, and significant differences also occur between the social organization of the Homeric and the classical periods. In what ways might these changes account for those in attitudes toward war?

Closely examine the work of Homer and of Aeschylus to bring out the divergences. Try to establish specific correspondences between certain social changes and certain attitudinal changes. Indicate how Aeschylus' attitude held the seeds of events in the next century.

Homer, *The Iliad*
Aeschylus, *The Persians* and *Seven Against Thebes*

Finley, *The World of Odysseus* and *The Ancient Greeks*
Kitto, *The Greeks*
Bowra, *The Greek Experience*
Dodd, *The Greeks and the Irrational*

(II)

The Polis and Reason

Many writers have suggested that the scale and social organization of the polis *deeply influenced modes of perception, explanation, and organization in Classical Greek thought. What are the major tenets of such an hypothesis? Is the argument convincing?*

Compare and try to synthesize the views of the authors listed below. Consider how well they account for the Greek predilection for limit, order, reason, and clarity by relating it to life in the *polis.*

Cornford, *From Religion to Philosophy* and *Principium Sapientiae*
McNeill, *The Rise of the West*
Bronstein, *Five Variations on the Theme of Japanese Painting* (variation III)
Bowra, *The Greek Experience*
Kitto, *The Greeks*

(II)

Millenia

Almost every period of history has experienced the fear of an end to civilization. Contemporary fear of the "bomb" and of ecological disaster updates a long history of similar predictions that, despite their preoccupation with the future, actually reveal much more about the society and the time that created them. How do these predictions compare with previous ones, and what does the comparison tell us about evolving societies?

Compare contemporary fears with medieval ones of the year 1000, with Indian theories of the holocaust, and with similar millenial fears of primitive cultures. Be as specific as possible in interpreting societies through their millenial fears.

Eliade, *Myth and Reality*
Campbell, *The Masks of God—Oriental Mythology*
Taylor, *The Medieval Mind*

(II)

The Social Origins of Religion

How much are religions the product of the unique inspirations of extraordinary individuals, and how much the result of social conditions that made *the individual and prepared the way for his vision?*

Consider social conditions at the time of the rise of a great religion—Judaism, Islam, or Christianity. Show how and in what ways the ideology and the material and spiritual needs of the time influenced the dogma and ritual of the new religion. Determine how the structure of society effected the structure of religion.

Weber, *Ancient Judaism* and *Sociology of Religion*

(I)

The Utopian Thought of Marx and Brown

The utopia of Marx and that of Brown are, according to their authors, not ideal projections but real possibilities. Although Marx's premises are economic and Brown's socio-psychological, both authors and their methodologies reflect social conditions of their times. Given their social contexts, which of these utopias is most reasonable? If both have serious defects, can these be traced to inescapable social conditions that produced false premises?

Analyze the two utopian theories and try to discern in their assumptions, method, and language the prejudices and intellectual trends that prevailed when they were written.

Brown, *Life Against Death*
Marx, *Selected Writings on Sociology and Social Philosophy* (ed. Bottomer)
Mannheim, *Ideology and Utopia*

(III)

Social Change and Art in Ancient Egypt

The difference between the sculpture styles of the Egyptian Old and Middle kingdoms often has been attributed to the changed status of the king, the experience of social anxiety, and the king's increased sense of responsibility for his subjects. How valid is this thesis?

Compare the royal portraits of these two periods to discover changed expression, idealization, and posture. State whether the differences can be explained in any way other than the hypothesis offered. If not, detail correlations between the new art and the new society.

Hauser, *The Social History of Art*
Frankfort, *The Ancient World*
Lloyd, *The Art of the Ancient Near East*

(I)

Ideas and Their Social Conditions

Durkheim proposes social structure as the origin of religious ideas, but Weber suggests that it is ideas like religion that are agents of human social development. What are the main divergences of these two thinkers? Whose position seems most reasonable?

In comparing these analyses of religion, place the authors in their historical and social contexts and show how much both content and methodology are the products of particular social milieus.

Durkheim, *Elementary Forms of the Religious Life*
Weber, *Sociology of Religion* and *The Religion of China*
Nisbet, *Emile Durkheim*

(III)

Moral Expectations and Social Conditions

Both Plato and the prophets of the Old Testament have a common radical intention—to impose new kinds of moral considerations on the exercise of political power. Although Plato and the prophets lived at roughly the same time, their thoughts developed in very different societies. How can you account for a similar rise in moral expectations in such different social environments?

In tackling this problem, decide whether important similarities in social situations were hidden behind apparent differences or whether it is necessary to qualify the Marxist view that thought is a direct product of social organization.

Weber, *Ancient Judaism*
Finley, *The Ancient Greeks*
Kitto, *The Greeks*
Plato, *The Republic*
Old Testament—books of Isaiah and of Amos

(III)

The Agrarian Theme in Modern Fiction

How do contemporary writers perceive agrarian society? Do they romanticize or attack it? Are the writers from the city or from the country, and what are their views of Gemeinschaft *and* Gesellschaft?

Choose a writer—Hesse, in this case—and analyze his agrarian motifs. Show how a study of the writer's social background illuminates his perception and treatment of these motifs.

Hesse, *Siddhartha; Demian;* and *Steppenwolf*
Marx, L., *The Machine in the Garden*
Toennies, *Community and Society*
Camenzia, *Hesse*

(II)

Geometry and Neolithic Societies

The Agrarian Revolution that led to Neolithic culture created stable communities, differentiated jobs, and the increasing organization of society. The art of this period is characterized by great stress on geometric forms and very organized composition. Is there any correlation between these two phenomena? If so, what kind, and how much?

Analyze the thesis that this style was a *result* of the agrarian economic and social experience. State whether it is based on facts or only on strong indications. If there is no conclusive evidence, decide whether you can support the thesis simply because of coincidence between a certain style and certain social conditions.

Hauser, *Social History of Art*
Gideion, *The Eternal Present: the Beginnings of Art*
Frankfort, *The Ancient World*
Childe, *What Happened in History*

(II)

Simmel's Social Context

Like any other form of knowledge, sociology is subject to the sociology of knowledge. What was the social context of Simmel's thought? Do its underlying assumptions, characteristic themes, and approaches reflect the concerns and intellectual styles of his age? If so, to what degree?

In exploring this problem, concentrate on how much of Simmel's work seems to be personal invention and how much seems to be the result of general attitudes of the people around him.

Wolff, *The Sociology of Georg Simmel*
Wolff, ed., *Essays on Sociology, Philosophy, and Aesthetics*

(III)

The Incest Taboo and Its Theorists

The incest taboo has fascinated innumerable theorists in sociology, anthropology, and psychology. What do theories and descriptions of the incest taboo reveal about the individuals who formulated them and the societies in which they were formulated?

Discuss theories of incest in relation to their authors' personal backgrounds and to the theoretical and cultural framework in which they appeared.

Freud, *Totem and Taboo*
Jones, *The Life and Work of Sigmund Freud*

Malinowski, *The Sexual Life of Savages*
Brown, *Taboo*
Mead, *Family*

(II)

Individualism, Portraits, and Central Authority

During periods of social cohesion because of strong central authority, common ideals, or pervasive faith, the cult of the individual and the art of portraiture seem to decline. What explanation can you offer for this phenomenon?

Approach this problem by studying the opposite case, when, during periods of social unrest, formentation, and conflicting authority, portraiture increases. Note the individuals that are portrayed, the faithfulness of the portrayal, the frequency and variety of portraits, and the subjects of portraits, whether special or anonymous.

McNeill, *The Rise of the West*
Janson, *History of Art*
Durant, *History of Civilization*

(I)

The Utopian Novel

The Utopian novel has had great impact on contemporary thought. What has been its importance over the last half century? What does the appearance of such novels indicate about society's self concept?

Compare *Looking Backward*, *Brave New World*, and *1984*. Show how these works are rooted in the fears, criticisms, and trends of the periods in which they were written. Indicate how their authors' social backgrounds and contexts had particular effects on the kind of utopia proposed.

Bellamy, *Looking Backward*
Orwell, *1984*
Huxley, *Brave New World*

(I)

The Church and Society

Changes in religious attitudes often are connected with major social changes, but it is hard to determine the actual causal relationship between the two. Using particular examples of religious literature, can you discern any part of such a relationship?

Compare sermons and religious treatises of today (from Southern Baptist churches, campuses, and urban churches) with those of Puritan New England and/or Medieval France. Analyze their content, theatrics, assumptions of efficacy, and acceptance of contemporary mores. Show how much they cater to rather than improve on society's self concept, and determine how much they reveal about the comparative power of the church in society.

Wilson, *Religion in Secular Society*
Yinger, *Sociology Looks at Religion*
Schneider, *The Puritan Mind*
Huizinga, *The Waning of the Middle Ages*

(II)

The Art of Classical and Hellenistic Societies

Artistic style paralleled the development of Greek society from the polis *to an empire spread across many continents. The compact, geometrical, disciplined work of the fifth and sixth centuries became spiraling, expanding, and very grand in scale. What connections can you see between changes in the scale structure of Greek society and changes in artistic style?*

Isolate changing elements of style and try to explain them by referring to specific changes in the social structure and identity of Ancient Greece.

Hauser, *A Social History of Art*
Boardman, *Greek Art*
Webster, *The Age of Hellenism*

(II)

Primitive Cosmologies

Primitive ritual and primitive belief frequently are society's attempts to grapple not only with natural threats but with the social environment through which action is governed. Exactly how is the structure of a primitive society reflected in its relationship to its gods and its universe?

Using a basic monograph on a particular primitive society, briefly describe the elements and stresses of its social structure that are apparent in its cosmology. Pay special attention to the nature of an hierarchical social structure and the relationships among age grades.

Kroeber, *A Handbook of the Indians of California*
Lowie, *The Crow Indians*
Evans-Pritchard, *The Nuer*

(III)

Two Views of the Crowd

In comparing the two works listed below, what major divergences can you see? How far is Ortega y Gasset a European, or German Ideologist and how far is Riesman an ideologist of American society?

Examine both the context and content of these books to see how the former affects the latter. Indicate how the authors' backgrounds affect their work and their particular reactions to the crowd.

Ortega y Gasset, *The Revolt of the Masses*
Riesman, *The Lonely Crowd*

(I)

Cosmologies, Cosmogonies, Society, and Geography

The way in which the emerging cultures of Egypt and Mesopotamia saw and explained the universe and its origins was closely connected with their land, their climate, and the development of their social structures. How well do a civilization's social context and geographical position explain its ideology? And how do the physical aspects of a civilization's land explain its society?

Analyze Egyptian and Mesopotamian cosmology and cosmogony. Test the interpretation stated above, and try to establish direct connections between geographical and social structure and characteristics.

Frankfort, *Before Philosophy* and *The Birth of Civilization in the Near East*
Cornford, *From Religion to Philosophy*

(I)

Marx and Social Reality

In two very different books—The German Ideology *and* The 18th Brumaire of Louis Bonaparte—*Marx attempted to gain insight into the social reality of history. How does he do so in each case? Which of his approaches seems most valid to you, and why?*

Show how subject affects approach in each work.

Indicate how Marx's general approach differs from current approaches to the analysis of social reality.

Marx and Engels, *Basic Writings on Politics and Philosophy* (ed. Feuer) and *The German Ideology*
Lefebvre, *The Sociology of Marx*
Marcuse, *Reason and Revolution*

(II)

The Future as Seen by Freud and Marx

Abstracting from detailed theoretical frameworks, both Freud and Marx predicted the state of future society. How does the methodology, style, and content of each prediction reflect the author's framework?

Determine whether these theories—one of which originates in psychiatry, the other in economics—are simply incompatible or entirely contradictory, and attribute your findings either to the frameworks or to the idiosyncratic development of the theories.

Freud, *Civilization and Its Discontents*
Marx, *Selected Writings* (ed. Bottomore)
Zeitling, *Ideology and the Development of Sociological Tradition*

(III)

Interdisciplinary, Philosophical, and Methodological Concerns of Sociology

Feed-Back Loops

The scientific feed-back loop is directly relevant to such crises as urban redevelopment and pollution, for social problems are not linear. What sociological concerns are involved in the resolution of problems like these and in the consequences of their solution? How does the feed-back loop indicate and affect these concerns?

Consider in particular the moral role of the social scientist and show how he himself is a part of the feed-back loop.

Bacon, *The Design of Cities*
Commoner, *Science and Survival*

(III)

The Validity of Marxist Athropology

Marxist anthropologists attempt to discover the underlying basis of the structure and function of primitive societies in economic factors, but traditional anthropologists de-emphasize these factors. How much do subsistence patterns and economic relationships actually affect both primitive and developed cultures?

Focus your discussion on channels of exchange and production within a society and their influence on specific social relationships.

Marx, *The Communist Manifesto*
Evans-Pritchard, *The Nuer*
Riesman, *Abundance for What?*

(II)

Weber's Rationalism

One of Weber's fundamental hypotheses is that the development of human society implies an increasing rationalization of man's thinking and conduct. Weber adduces the Reformation and Puritanism as examples. How valid is the hypothesis, and how well do the examples support it?

Having read some of Weber's work, explore his uses of rationalism and decide how accurate the preceding characterization really is.

Weber, *The Protestant Ethic and the Spirit of Capitalism*
Icheiser, "Six Meanings of the Term Irrational," *Sociologie Internationalis*, number 6, 1968
Gerth and Mills, ed., *From Max Weber*
Freund, *The Sociology of Max Weber*

(III)

The Morality of Power

Russell distinguishes between personal morality —based on individual conscience—and power morality, an elitist code based on obedience to some form of political, legal, or religious power. How personal is personal morality? Are elements of power morality inherent to it? Does it lead to power morality?

Examine the original tenets of the Christian ethic and compare it with later developments. Determine whether and how the original personal ethic contained the seeds of a power morality for the Church.

Russell, *Power*
Fremantle, *Papal Encyclicals*, pp. 126-129

(III)

Social Rationales for Punishment

Should our dealings with crime rely so heavily on punishment? Does such an approach reform the criminal or simply provide revenge for the victim and society? Does it benefit the solidarity of the punishing society, or does it dehumanize?

Examine the terminology and contents of the U.S. Penal Code and try to establish correlations between severity of punishment and crime rates. Base your argument on facts and support the values voiced in the works below that seem most reasonable.

Camus, "Reflections on the Guillotine," in *Resistance, Rebellion, and Death*
Mead, "The Psychology of Punitive Justice," *American Journal of Sociology*, March, 1918
Bedam, *The Death Penalty in America*
Report of the National Advisory Commission on Civil Disorders

(II)

Sociologists on Sociology

One of the sociologist's most important tasks is to analyze his discipline. How do such analyses differ? What kinds of questions do sociologists most frequently ask in this context?

Show how the three sociologists listed below differ in their basic concepts of sociology. Explain what Berger means by humanistic sociology and what attitude Mills thinks the sociologist should adopt. Show how Parsons' essay rebuts some objections to scientific sociology.

Berger, *Invitation to Sociology*
Mills, *The Sociological Imagination*
Parsons, *Essays in Sociological Theory*

(II)

Durkheim's Theory of Ritual

How valid is Durkheim's functional theory of religious ritual? Specifically, how is Durkheim's theory undermined by its retriction to religious *ritual rather than other kinds?*

Indicate this theory's contribution to the sociology of religion and to sociology in general. Decide whether it is possible to apply this theory to secular, modern rituals.

Durkheim, *The Elementary Forms of Religious Life*
Nisbet, *Emile Durkheim*
"Ritual," in the *International Encyclopedia of the Social Sciences*

(II)

Social Analysis and Political Economy

A non-Marxist approach to social analysis need not lead two authors to the some conclusions. How do Lipset's and Galbraith's prescriptions for change differ, and how does each author stand in relation to Marxist analysis?

Show why Lipset has been called a defender of liberal society and Galbraith a critic of the affluent society. Decide whether they are writing about the same society, and explain why change is not an integral part of their analyses.

Lipset, *Political Man*
Galbraith, *The New Industrial State*

(I)

Protestant and German

How do Marx and Weber approach religion, and what do each of them say about the relationship between religion and socio-economic conditions?

In bringing out the great differences between Marx and Weber, comment on the ways in which their theories of religion reflect their views on the relationship between ideology of any kind and social phenomena in general.

Marx, *The German Ideology*
Weber, *The Protestant Ethic and the Spirit of Capitalism*
Manheim, *Ideology and Utopia*
Nisbet, *The Sociological Tradition*

(II)

Social Structure and Religion

Theories that relate social structure and religion sometimes assume that religion is an integral part of any social system because it functions as a reflection of the social group's corporate identity, as a symbolic representation of social values, and as a projective ratification of the existing structure of social relationships. Are these functional assumptions valid? Exactly how does religion relate to social structure?

Study the influence of a particular religious belief on social control or some other aspect of the social structure. Include analyses of the extent to which beliefs and practices seem to influence the behavior of individuals and of the generally accepted association of beliefs and rites with social structure.

Wallace, *Religion: An Anthropological View*
Swanson, *Birth of the Gods*
Durkheim, *The Elementary Forms of the Religious Life*

(III)

The Social Assumptions of Living Space

The spaces in which we live are the products of more than technology, economics, and simple architecture. How does such space reflect our social assumptions?

Examine the visual differences between the living space of an urban and that of a non-urban society and show how they reflect differences in social interaction and in assumed social values.

Willgo, *Cities and Space*
Rudofski, *Architecture Without Architects*
Wright, *The Living City*
Neutra, *Survival Through Design*

(II)

A Christian View of the Structure of Society

How and where does Christianity legitimize and/ or condemn the inequality of human society? Why does it not encourage the believer to change his (low) status and escape poverty? What are the roles of the alms-giver and the legitimate beggar?

Closely examine the writings of St. Augustine to see how his religious viewpoint influences his view of the structure and function of society in general. Distinguish between the religious and the social factors which influenced his thought.

Deane, *The Political and Social Ideas of St. Augustine*
Paolucci, ed., *St. Augustine's Political Writings*
Ullman, *A History of Political Thought: The Middle Ages*

(II)

The Uses and Possibilities of Cross-national Sociology.

Cross-national, as well as cross-cultural studies naturally are essential to the construction of sociological theory. How well do they point out the constants of social experience, the common ground that underlies national and cultural social differences? What factors inhibit the validity of such studies?

Show how the general scope of Durkheim's and of Weber's work contributes to the validity of their studies. Examine how social and personal factors can limit such work.

Durkheim, *Suicide*
Weber, *Sociology of Religion*
Eliade, *The Two and the One*
Stein, "Cross-national Sociology, an Introductory Note," *Transactions, Sixth World Congress of Sociology*, volume I, 1966

(III)

The Consequences of War Technology

How does the technology of war change its character? What is the impact of war's organization on the soldiers and the society that fight it?

Compare the data you can collect through library research and interviews with veterans concerning the different technologies and effects of the last two world wars.

Preston, Wise, and Werner, *Men in Arms*
Andreski, *Military Sociology*

(II)

A Critical Summary of the Uses of Mathematics in Sociology

How are mathematics currently used in sociology? What future trends are clear? What, exactly, are the limits of its use in sociological studies?

Present a critical discussion and summary of the book and article cited below.

Coleman, *Mathematical Sociology*
Gossman, "Gravity Models and Sociology," *Washington Journal of Sociology*, March, 1969

(II)

Contemporary Applications of Marx

Recently discovered, Marx's early philosophical manuscripts have furnished "revisionists" with a text for designing a Marxism relevant to the "human" problems of our time. Have contemporary Marxist humanists illuminated Marx's ideas? Or have they distorted them beyond recognition?

Consider how Marx and his successors treated the problem of alienation. Show how this treatment has been recast to apply exclusively to contemporary socio-psychological problems.

Kolokowski, *Toward a Marxist Humanism*
Bottomore, *Karl Marx: The Early Writings*
Marcuse, *One Dimensional Man*

(III)

Literature as Sociology

Telling views of society appear in literature that describes the interaction of the individual and society. What is the role of the novel or play as sociology? How does lack of sociological training affect an author's ability to reach conclusions about society?

Discuss the views of society presented in the works cited below. Show how each reflects the milieu of its author. Be specific about the ways in which these works present keys to society, its effects on the individual, and its changes.

Fitzgerald, *The Great Gatsby*
Dreiser, *Sister Carrie*
Larcom, *A New England Girlhood*

(I)

Berger and the Sociology of Religion

Spiritual and religious values have become increasingly important in our technological society. How does the sociologist of religion explain this phenomenon? How does his treatment of it differ from that produced in other disciplines? In sum, what are the major operative features of the sociology of religion?

Consider Berger's work. Compare his approach and emphasis to Weber's. Show how their divergent theories illuminate the history of the sociology of religion as well as the changing patterns of Western thought.

Berger, *Rumor of Angels* and *Sacred Canopy*
Robertson, ed., *Sociology of Religion*
Weber, *Sociology of Religion*

(II)

Objectivity and the Social Sciences

Many writers have considered the demand that sociologists be objective and view their field as the scientist would the natural world. What are the moral and epistemological questions that this demand raises?

Discuss the meaning and effects of *value neutrality*. State whether it is possible, and how its absence affects science. Describe the *pseudo-value neutrality* of scientists who value the neutral stance but make known their prejudices by the subjects they choose and the ways they treat that subject. State whether the scientist has a responsibility to society and how this responsibility affects the need for value neutrality.

Chomsky, *The Responsibility of Intellectuals* and "Objectivity and Liberal Scholarship," in *American Power and the New Mandarins*
Meehan, *Value Judgment and Social Science*
Mills, *Power, Politics, and People* and *The Sociological Imagination*

(III)

Society and the Job Market

Changes in the job market, usually a concern of economics, also can indicate trends in the larger society. The mass of job applicants and positions of certain kinds can tell us about society's changing needs. How does the ratio of demand and supply for a specific job indicate particular structural problems of society?

Study the employment sections of newspapers at five year intervals over the last thirty years and note changes. Use statistical yearbooks and interviews with employment agencies to support your findings. Try to relate particular trends in job offers and applications to particular, primarily social changes.

Hughes, *Men and Their Work*
Durkheim, *The Division of Labor*
Park, "Human Migration and the Marginal Man," *American Journal of Sociology*, 1928

(II)

Psychosis in Literature

Literature often provides the most vivid and illuminating descriptions of psychological disorders, for psychotic symtoms often are crucial to an author's characters. What aspects of mental pathology does literature emphasize? How?

Compare literary and clinical studies of paranoia, or severe character disorders. Show how fictional studies can be useful to an understanding of mental health and disease.

Stone and Stone, *The Abnormal Personality Through Literature*
Kesey, *One Flew Over the Cuckoo's Nest*
Kaplan, *The Inner World of Mental Illness*

(II)

The Social Factors of Perception

Perception is culturally conditioned, despite revolutions in media and expansion of knowledge. How does the social structure perform such conditioning? What are some of the final effects?

Use Mathiessen's book as a guide. Show how social factors like class, bureaucracy, and interaction influence not only the ways we perceive society, the world, objects, and time but also how much of them we perceive.

Mathiessen, *Under the Mountain Wall*
Mumford, *Technics and Civilization*
McLuhan, *The Gutenberg Galaxy*

(II)

Capital Punishment and the Crime Rate

Recently the Office of the Attorney-General of Massachusetts stated, "Crime is on the upswing in the U.S. Now is not the time to abolish the death penalty." How valid are the statistical correlations on which this statement is based? What evidence is there both for and against the positive relationship of the crime rate to abolition of the death penalty?

Use contemporary studies on capital punishment as well as federal statistics on the increase of crime. Relate the fundamental arguments for and against the death penalty and analyze the sociological validity of their assumptions.

Knudten, *Criminological Controversies*
Sutherland and Cressey, *Principles of Criminology*
Vold, *Theoretical Criminology*

(III)

Society in Philosophical Perspective

How does the philosopher's analysis of people's motivations differ from the sociologist's? What are the specific differences of approach? Do they give different answers to the same questions, or do they raise entirely different questions?

Examine the work of a philosopher who has developed a comprehensive theory of society—either Plato (*The Republic*) or Hobbes (*Leviathan*). Decide whether he tries to explain society and solve all moral problems or uses society simply to illustrate his theories. Show how much these theories rely on observation and how much on abstract logic.

(II)

The Ethics of Participant Observation

The participant observer gains the trust of his subjects in order to gather certain kinds of information. In such cases, the line between use and abuse of the information, between discretion and indiscretion becomes very thin. When and how does the contribution that a sociological study makes justify ethically dubious or dangerous means of gathering information? What guidelines should the social scientist observe when he must violate the rights and privacy of human beings?

Examine participant observation studies and criticisms of sociological methods. Try to reconcile the informational needs of the social scientist with the legal and moral rights of the individual.

Attempt to establish rules for measuring the worth of a social study and relating it to the costs it incurs.

Liebow, *Tally's Corner*
Whyte, *Street Corner Society*
Agee and Walker, *Let Us Now Praise Famous Men*

(III)

Research and Interaction

When a social scientist begins to define and study what he perceives as a "problem," the essence and the manifestations of that problem can change radically. Exactly how does the social scientist's intervention affect a specific "social problem"?

Concentrate on two areas: the changes that occur in the conceptual definition of the problem and the changes that occur in the real problem because of the interrelations of the researcher and his subject or subjects. Determine whether social research is capable of objectivity under these conditions.

Seeley, "Implications and Appendices—Americanization of the Unconscious," in *Crestwood Heights*
Gerth and Mills, ed., *From Max Weber* (especially "Politics As a Vocation" and "Science As a Vocation")

(II)

"A Tree Grows in Brooklyn" as Social Criticism

Many students of the city accept A Tree Grows in Brooklyn *as a classic portrait of city life. What specific aspects of city life does Smith characterize carefully, and which ones does she neglect? What are her attitudes toward Industrialization, traffic, ghettos, and the prospects of urban growth and improvement?*

Use the reference works listed below as a starting point in your analysis. Try to relate the attitudes expressed in the book to the author's socio-historical context.

Marx, L., *The Machine in the Garden*
Wilson, *The Arts in Society*
Smith, *A Tree Grows in Brooklyn*

(I)